Usable Privacy and Security
in Online Public Services

Esther Ruiz Ben • Margit Scholl

Usable Privacy and Security in Online Public Services

 Springer

Esther Ruiz Ben
Faculty of Business, Computing and Law
TH Wildau
Wildau, Germany

Margit Scholl
Faculty of Business, Computing and Law
TH Wildau
Wildau, Germany

ISBN 978-3-031-43382-5   ISBN 978-3-031-43383-2   (eBook)
https://doi.org/10.1007/978-3-031-43383-2

This Springer imprint is published by the registered company Springer Nature Switzerland AG
The registered company address is: Gewerbestrasse 11, 6330 Cham, Switzerland

Paper in this product is recyclable.

Preface

This book is a unique guide for the implementation of usable, privacy-compliant and secure online services in the area of e-government. Departing from the clarification of basic concepts of usability, data privacy and cybersecurity, the book provides clear explanations of different methods (quantitative, qualitative and mixed methods) to apply in the practice of designing, developing and evaluating online public services considering both usability criteria as well as data privacy and IT security compliance. Several examples and exercises as well as awareness raising measures that can serve as orientation for practitioners and for teaching purposes are included. A concise glossary of terms and recommendations of further readings are also covered in the book.

Aims and Scope

Over the last decade, usability has become a crucial requirement for developing interfaces along with technical skills for all the tasks of any product and service development team. The importance of data privacy and information security has become crucial as well due to the increasing connectivity and complexities of devices and systems in which interfaces are integrated. Increasing data privacy and information security requirements constitutes a major challenge for developing usable products and online services.

Both usability and data privacy and information security constitute basic essential requirements for developing online public services aiming to achieve digital citizenship, as defined in the EU Digital Targets for 2030.[1]

---

[1] https://ec.europa.eu/info/strategy/priorities-2019-2024/europe-fit-digital-age/europes-digital-decade-digital-targets-2030_en. Accessed 14 Sep 2022

However, combining these frequently contradictory aspects of software development is insufficiently considered in practice as well as in curricula. Usable privacy and information security are by their nature interdisciplinary. Moreover, the development of online public services requires bureaucratic and legal knowledge as well as awareness about the diversity of users' digital skills and needs as citizens. Our book contributes to introducing these interdisciplinary skills into this still neglected area of e-government.

This book is essential for everyone who is interested in understanding how the principles of usable privacy and information security can contribute to a design that ensures that the needs of the citizens in e-government have been properly met. Therefore, this work offers guidelines regarding the participation of users from diverse backgrounds in the development of usable designs for secure and safe online public services. The book intends to provide guidelines for a minimalist, accessible, useful and efficient design of interfaces that enable users to interact easily with online public services while understanding data privacy and information security requirements and risks. It is important to understand that guidelines also need to be reviewed and updated – which is why the continuous improvement process is an integral part of this book.

The scope of the book is not restricted to students and academics of computer science or human-computer interaction. Practitioners from different disciplines working in the implementation of online public services can benefit from the guidelines and examples provided in the text as well. It is written as a practice-oriented textbook that aims to include comprehensive coverage of usability, data privacy and information security topics. Moreover, it is also up-to-date in the implementation of the single digital gateway regulation in the European Union at the time this book is going to press.

Main Emphasis

The main emphasis of this book is on the application of usability methods for designing, developing and evaluating online public services considering data privacy and information security compliance. Therefore, the first chapters will cover the concepts of usable privacy and information security, followed by explanations of the specific challenges of considering these concepts in e-government and online public services environments. The last chapters are more extensive and focus on the implementation of usable security methods with examples and exercises. The examples and exercises included in these chapters have been recently used in teaching and are up-to-date. They have been tested several times. The last chapter includes references and a glossary of terms as well as recommendations for further readings that can be used for teaching purposes.

Main Target Groups (Benefits for the Target Groups), Prerequisites for Understanding and Relation to Other Publications

The main target groups are students and teachers as well as practitioners. Departing from the idea that usable privacy and information security are necessarily interdisciplinary in nature, the book is not exclusively restricted to specific disciplines. The intended audience is persons interested in understanding the principles of usable privacy and information security and in how they can contribute to the design, development and evaluation of online public services that meet the needs of citizens. Therefore, possibilities of awareness-raising are also shown. This book is written in a concise and comprehensible language, illustrated with pictures and tables, enabling a fast understanding of the covered concepts, and includes a glossary of terms intended to clarify the terminology used for a broad nonspecialised audience. Broad audiences can benefit from finding explanations of numerous terms that are sometimes difficult to grasp hiding behind acronyms. Moreover, the book provides an up-to-date overview of the data privacy and information security regulations in national and multinational e-government environments (i.e. the Online Access Act and single digital gateway in the context of the European Union) that practitioners must confront while applying usable privacy and security methods in the development of online public services. These regulations and promising digitisation targets at national and multinational levels remain unnoticed by some citizens for whom they are also created. This book intends to also benefit these unaware audiences, contributing to narrowing digital gaps and supporting trust in e-government with explanations about the development and implementation of multinational digital targets affecting the usage of online public services.

Wildau, Germany   Esther Ruiz Ben
                                                                                                           Margit Scholl

Contents

Chapter 1
The Concept of Usable Privacy and Information Security

This chapter introduces the concept of usable data privacy and information security. The concept of usable data privacy and information security situates the user on the focus of designing privacy and information security measures for IT products and services. As Schmitt et al. (2017: 3) emphasise, the term "user" in the usable privacy and security concept not only refers to software users but also to IT developers. These clarifications should also ensure that security and data protection measures are implemented in a comprehensible and effective, clear and easy and accessible form. In addition, the constant increase in digital devices results in a growing number of security and data protection measures. These are a permanent challenge for users because they are requested to take decisions and actions about passwords and password management, virus scanners, malware, communication and data encryption, etc. Additionally, not all users recognise the significance and importance of the various security concepts in the web and applications or the consequences of making incorrect decisions. User centricity and the developers' acknowledgement that "users are not the enemies" (see Adams and Sasse 1999) are therefore central in the concept of usable privacy and security.

1.1 The Concept of Usable Privacy and Security

The concept of usable privacy and security refers to the centrality of users in the design of secure and user-friendly digital tools or infrastructures. The departing idea is that privacy, security and user friendliness are not mutually exclusive characteristics of an information system (Sasse et al. 2016; Reuter et al. 2022). Research in this area is based on the assumption that data privacy and security can be partially controlled from a user perspective through internal mechanisms or active engagement by users themselves, such as consent, correction or choice, as well as external instruments such as laws or technological self-regulation (Tavani 2007).

The concept of user centricity in security systems was already acknowledged in the nineteenth century by Kerckhoffs (1883) in his work about military cryptography (Reuter et al. 2022: 2). Kerckhoffs (1883) defined six principles in the late nineteenth century, of which the second and the third emphasise the idea that a secret can be a breakage source and therefore should be kept to a minimum (Petitcolas 2011).

Petitcolas (2011)[1] notes that Shannon later defined the maxim "the enemy knows the system". Both Kerckhoffs' principles and Shannon's maxim constitute basic IT privacy and security concepts opposed to the idea of privacy and security by obscurity and obfuscation. Kerckhoffs' security principles are important for usable privacy and security because they already consider the importance of information systems' ease of use. Later, in the mid-1990s of the last century, usable security began to be established as a research field focusing on passwords and email communication risks. These research focuses departed from Adams' and Sasse's (1999) as well as Whiten's and Tygar's (1999) pioneering ideas. Similarly, usable privacy's trajectory as a research field was boosted by the rapid development of the World Wide Web in the late years of the last century and the work of Cranor and Garfinkel (2005).

Usable privacy and security scholars emphasise the fact that secure systems rely on humans to perform and complete security functions or privacy rules. Cranor (2008) calls this the "human in the loop". Relying on humans and their diverse perspectives and knowledge means confronting human errors in the performance and completion of security functions and privacy rules. Software developers and designers must therefore explore the reasons for security failures in the interactions between humans and computer systems. The privacy and security of information systems originally ignored the basic usability aspects of effectiveness, efficiency and satisfaction. These aspects have increasingly become important in the development of information systems and have led to the conceptualisation of usable privacy and security in academic and practitioner environments. If privacy and security of information systems ignore the skills and understandings of the users as well as the contexts of use, privacy and security can become a barrier to accomplishing basic systems requirements. This situation can lead to risks in which users may avoid activating security measures (Schmitt et al. 2017). Information systems are designed expecting active user involvement in accomplishing privacy and security

---

[1]The six principles of Kerckhoffs cited by Petitcolas (2011) are as follows:

1. *The system must be substantially, if not mathematically, undecipherable.*
2. *The system must not require secrecy and can be stolen by the enemy without causing trouble (what is currently referred to as Kerckhoffs' principle).*
3. *It must be easy to communicate and remember the keys without requiring written notes, and it must also be easy to change or modify the keys with different participants.*
4. *The system should be compatible with telegraph communication.*
5. *The system must be portable, and its use must not require more than one person.*
6. *Finally, regarding the circumstances in which such system is applied, it must be easy to use and must neither require stress of mind nor the knowledge of a long series of rules.*

requirements[2] without considering users' understandings, needs and contexts of use. However, security and usability researchers have long been aware of the usability of privacy and security requirements in information systems (Garfinkel 2005).

Whitten and Tygar (1999) showed, for example, that the user interfaces for PGP 5.0 were not sufficient to make computers securely usable for laypersons. These authors identify four necessary qualities for the usability of security software (Whitten and Tygar 1999: 170).[3] Later revisions of the pioneering work of Whitten and Tygar (1999) suggest generalising the concept of security software to all types of software and avoiding concentrating only on disclosure aspects of security posing the same importance to further security aspects (integrity, availability and audit). A third important critique of these pioneering ideas is the question of how "visible" security should be for users. While Whitten (2004), for example, recommends making security visible and managed by the user, Garfinkel suggested, on the contrary, making security invisible (Garfinkel 2005). Garfinkel's argument against visibility of security for users is based upon the assumption that every user will make the right decision under visibility of security circumstances. Garfinkel hypothesised, however, that machines may make better security decisions than humans. Dykstra (2020) contends that invisible security, while not a monolithic solution for security in information systems, could support those users who even struggle with usable security. This question about the visibility of security and how much action should be expected from users to protect their data has until today been controversial. These contrary scholar positions are related to differing methods and perspectives of usable privacy and information security differently involving users in the development of privacy and security of information systems. We will come to this question in Chap. 5.

In addition to these models of usable privacy and information security and trying to overcome the multidisciplinary contradictory interpretations about privacy and security in information systems, Lederer et al. (2004) propose concentrating on the formulation of guidelines for designers of privacy and security. Lederer et al. identified five major privacy pitfalls grouped into two categories: first, understanding, including obscuring potential information flow and obscuring actual information flow, and second, action which includes an emphasis on configuration over action, lacks coarse-grained control and inhibits established practice. To confront these pitfalls, Lederer et al. (2004) suggest different strategies, such as making explicit the basic scope of potential disclosures to help users understand their

---

[2]For example, users are required to be informed about a system's data processing practices; to give consent, provided with a mechanism to withdraw consent; or to give access to their own data – including options for data portability and data deletion (Schaub and Cranor 2020).

[3]"Definition: Security software is usable if the people who are expected to use it:

1. are reliably made aware of the security tasks they need to perform;
2. are able to figure out how to successfully perform those tasks;
3. do not make dangerous errors; and
4. are sufficiently comfortable with the interface to continue using it".

potential audience or informing users when someone else is searching for them. Users learn with this strategy who is obtaining what information. Several guiding methods and tools have been developed and optimised for different contexts since these early stages of usable privacy and security with multidisciplinary contributions, for example, human-centred design, usability, security or psychology.

Closely related to usable privacy and security are the concepts of user centricity, user-centred design or human-centred design, which have a long trajectory in information systems (Ritter et al. 2014). Human-centred design is integrated in the International Organization for Standardization's (ISO) ergonomics guidelines of human-system interaction,[4] for example. In the EU, there are also human-centred standards, including specific ones for OPS, as we will explain in Chap. 4.

In recent decades, the concept of usable privacy and security has evolved, including topics such as the development of usable privacy and security tools (i.e. privacy-enhancing technologies (PETs); transparency-enhancing technologies (TETs)) (Zimmermann 2015), research on dark patterns (sludges), the usage of icons, visualisation instruments and games, the consideration of developers and software engineers as a target user group or the risks derived from home-office tasks due to the pandemic circumstances, which also challenge the conceptualisation of privacy and its legislation in the intersection with digital technologies (Reuter et al. 2022).

Another assumption in usable privacy and security research is that technological self-regulation and the legal basis of information systems are often deficient (Tavani and Moor 2001), so different instruments are necessary to address the negative consequences of these systems' deficits. It is also expected that users are most responsible for maintaining their own privacy[5] and that they can be supported to become "sovereign users" of online services. Internal mechanisms of data protection from the user's perspective thus gain importance. However, users are often confronted with difficult decisions about the extent to which they disclose private information to access and use online services (Dinev and Hart 2006). Moreover, not all users want to think about security whenever they use IT systems. In addition, the form of information transfer to support decision-making about data protection and security that service providers must offer online (s. Chap. 3) is often nontransparent and misleading (see "dark patterns": Rieger and Sienders 2020). Due to their complexity and length, information on privacy and security requires considerable time and expertise from users (Park 2013; McDonald and Cranor 2008) and is usually not read (Sunyaev et al. 2015; Schaub and Cranor 2020). Thus, an important aspect to consider in usable privacy and security is the role of trust in the interaction between users and providers of online services. Research on information privacy and

---

[4]ISO 9241-210:2019(en) Ergonomics of human-system interaction – Part 210: Human-centred design for interactive systems.

https://www.iso.org/obp/ui/#iso:std:iso:9241:-210:ed-2:v1:en (accessed 7 Feb 2023)

[5]For a detailed explanation of the concept of IT-privacy, see van den Hoven et al. (2016) in https://plato.stanford.edu/entries/it-privacy/ (accessed 2 Dec 2022).

security has included both the conception of users as the "weakest link" and the idea that the development of more usable privacy and security would benefit users' correct usage of privacy and security (Kirlappos and Sasse 2014). However, Kirlappos and Sasse (2014) argue that the implicit assumption in both conceptions is not sustained by the fact that users seek efficiency in their daily lives, so that the less they have to think about security, the better for them. Thus, trust between the users and the internet and service providers becomes crucial. As we will explain in Chap. 4, trust is a particularly important usable privacy and security challenge of e-government and OPS. Related concepts to this are data privacy by design and by default, which we will explain in Chap. 4.

Regarding the theoretical background of usable privacy and security, some common ideas come from behavioural economics and decision research (Sunstein 2016; Thaler and Sunstein 2008; Acquisti 2004; Acquisti et al. 2017). This background focuses on the reactions of individuals to messages related (mostly) to consumption or service usage. The so-called nudges play an important role in this research background. Numerous studies have revealed how interfaces and services can be designed to circumvent potentially harmful privacy and security decisions (Chiasson et al. 2008; Acquisti 2009; Wang et al. 2014; Almuhimedi et al. 2015; Acquisti et al. 2017). Concepts such as "weak", "libertarian" or "soft" paternalism from behavioural economics form the theoretical basis of these studies. Two systems of thought are identified in nudge theory: First, the intuitive system, which functions automatically, quickly, unconsciously and continuously, takes in environmental information actively and associatively. Second, the reflective system only acts actively in more complex decisions. This second system processes information in a more thorough, differentiated, controlled and thus slower and more strenuous way. Both systems work together, which not only brings advantages of mutual control but also disadvantages because the weakness of the first system is that simple problem-solving mechanisms ("heuristics") can be adopted with potential false conclusions. The weakness in the second system is the adoption of erroneous conclusions ("bias") from the first system, which are then sometimes incorporated without correction. This leads to bias (Kahneman 2012: 32 ff.; Fuhrberg 2019: 79).

The term nudging goes back to the practices of government regulation studied by Thaler and Sunstein (2011). Nudging refers to the targeted application of behavioural science findings to behavioural change. So-called nudges are used as instruments and empirically based policy processes ("test-learn-adapt") (Thorun et al. 2021).

Based on these theoretical ideas, Thaler and Sunstein (2008) distinguish between four "heuristics" (representativeness/similarity heuristics; recognition heuristics; anchoring heuristics; availability heuristics) and eight "biases" (status quo, procrastination, inertia; salience, conjunction, confirmation; self-serving; hindsight; social influences, norms and cooperation; framing) that have been empirically identified. These elements form the basis for "nudges" (Thaler and Sunstein 2008). Nudges are used by governments (OECD 2017) in policy to enforce social interventions or to achieve behavioural change (Gigerenzer 2015; Fuhrberg 2019).

However, study results state that negative nudges, sanctions and even the threat of punishment are currently not adequate means to achieve changes in people's behaviour; changes in the direction of increasing information security must be considered. This shows the great power of designers in democratic societies and the responsibility of the authorities in building digital public services.

In the field of usable data privacy and security, so-called security nudges are being developed to replace automated users' habits with active conscious decisions. Nudge elements in the decision architecture are intended to help consumers become aware of data protection issues in specific situations. Unconscious decisions of the first system (see the above behavioural economics theory) are subjected to a cognitive review and replaced by decisions of the second system that account for long-term costs and benefits (Acquisti 2009). Beck (2014) criticises the empirical basis from which the "heuristics" and "biases" stem, contending that subjects are provoked into bias. "Sludging" or even "dark patterns" – the negative implementation of nudges – are particularly important to be avoided in the context of the necessary users' consent to process and transfer or save digital private data.

From the "positive" perspectives of nudging implementation in digital environments, various tools (privacy-enhancing technologies – PETs) (Bertino 2020) have been empirically investigated to improve the user experience of privacy and security in online services (e.g. in the medical field: Brüggemann et al. 2016). These PETs include different elements, such as simple visual privacy warning indicators (e.g. a lock image in the browser navigation page while using encrypted connections) or more complex elements (e.g. anonymisation software, cookie management software or privacy statements) (Xu et al. 2012). However, these tools have little added value due to their lack of focus on the actual different needs or competences of users. These tools do not communicate to users what personal data are collected from them and in what context (Sunyaev et al. 2015). Moreover, transparency-enhancing technologies (TETs) aim to overcome PET bias and emphasise the basic principles of transparency. We will return to the topic of nudging later in Chap. 5.

In summary, usable privacy and security practices are supported by functionality tools (i.e. PET and TET nudges) to steer users into certain "safe" ways of use. While PETs can offer valuable mechanisms to protect users from unwanted data disclosure, they do not provide suitable support in the context of user profiling and personalisation in internet services characterised by high information asymmetry. TETs emphasise the transparency principle[6] and provide users with information regarding providers' data collection, analysis and usage, aiming to reduce internet services' information asymmetry (Zimmermann 2015).

An important aspect to consider in the implementation of these tools is their adaptation to different levels of users' competence and knowledge so that users can understand privacy mechanisms and security risks themselves and make informed choices. Mills (2022) proposes the personalisation of nudges to better acknowledge users' heterogeneity (Mills 2022). In the next section, we focus on the general

---

[6]https://eur-lex.europa.eu/eli/reg/2016/679/oj (accessed 2 Dec 2022)

application of nudging in usable privacy and security. In Chap. 5, we will concretise this general application of nudging in methods to implement in the development of usable and secure OPS.

1.2 Nudging and Usable Privacy and Security

Usable privacy and security scholars use the differentiation between "heuristics" and "biases" proposed by Tversky and Kahneman (1981) as well as the concepts of incomplete and asymmetric information to classify the barriers that people must overcome when making data privacy and security decisions on the internet (Acquisti et al. 2017).

The concepts of incomplete and asymmetric information refer to the situation between actors who have unequal access to relevant information about IT security. For example, the information of hackers is different from that of users or IT service providers. In this asymmetric situation, heuristics are the application of general short rules to confront the uncertainty and challenges of data protection or IT security.

The concept of cognitive and behavioural biases refers to systematic errors in judgements or behaviour regarding data protection and cybersecurity. Biases are classified into seven types (Acquisti et al. 2017). The first type is anchoring, or the use of short information in decision-making processes, even if this information is not necessarily helpful. Second, loss avoidance is related to the phenomenon that people value their personal data more when they have it under control than when they believe they have lost it (Acquisti et al. 2017: 8). The third type of bias is the so-called framing effect. This effect occurs when certain options are expressed more positively than others. For example, if one privacy measure is presented as better than another, users will judge the options as more secure or insecure. This can also influence users' voluntariness to protect their privacy. The fourth type of bias, hyperbolic discounting, refers to the trade-off between the effort it takes to implement a privacy measure versus not implementing the measure and accepting the consequences. For example, not installing privacy software may save time and effort, but the threat to potential hackers is greater in the long run (Acquisti et al. 2017: 9). Optimistic biases are the fifth bias type and refer to the underestimations that users make about the consequences of a data protection attack loss. The overestimation of one's own knowledge about the consequences of data protection attacks also belongs to this fifth bias type. Postcompletion errors are the sixth type of bias, and in data protection and IT security, they also refer to the steps that are necessary in data protection measures on the internet but go unnoticed. Examples are forgetting to log out of systems or cleaning browser history when personal data are shared. The seventh type of bias is the "status quo bias". In the context of data protection and IT security, this type of bias refers to users' preference for existing "default" options. For example, users assume that they are well protected if they select these existing options. This is also because information about data protection risks is often difficult to find, understand or read. In addition, default options are an important mechanism to manage uncertainty about preferences (Acquisti et al. 2017).

Nudging in data privacy and security is not free from controversy. The abovementioned nudging dimensions can support the digital sovereignty of users. On the other hand, these dimensions can also be used to support the interests of service providers on the internet without taking user interests or needs into account. So-called dark patterns are nudges that manipulate the actions of users in the interest of service providers. Sludges refer to the negative aspects of nudging. We will return to nudging in relation to usable privacy and security in Chap. 5, concretising the specific methods applied to OPS access and usage.

1.3   Summary

- The concept of usable privacy and security refers to the centrality of users in the design of secure and user-friendly digital tools or infrastructures.
- Usable privacy and security scholars emphasise the fact that secure systems rely on humans to perform and complete security functions or privacy rules.
- The question about how much action should be expected from users to protect their data has until today been controversial.
- Due to users' differing digital skills and attitudes towards learning and activating privacy and security tools, trust in online service providers is a particularly important usable privacy and security challenge of the e-government and OPS.
- In recent decades, the concept of usable privacy and security has evolved, including topics such as the development of usable privacy and security tools (i.e. privacy-enhancing technologies (PETs); transparency-enhancing technologies (TETs)) (Zimmermann 2015), research on dark patterns (sludges), the usage of icons, visualisation instruments and games and the consideration of developers and software engineers as a target user group.
- Usable privacy and security practices are supported by functionality tools (i.e. PET and TET nudges) to steer users into certain "safe" ways of use.
- While PETs can offer valuable mechanisms to protect users from unwanted data disclosure, they do not provide suitable support in the context of user profiling and personalisation in internet services characterised by high information asymmetry. TETs emphasise the transparency principle.[7]

---

[7] https://eur-lex.europa.eu/eli/reg/2016/679/oj (accessed 2 Dec 2022)

1.4 Examples and Exercises

1.4.1 Examples

- **Secure multi-party computation (SMPC)** is a generic cryptographic method enabling distributed parties to jointly analyse big data without revealing private information (i.e. Zhao et al. 2019).
- **Homomorphic encryption** is a cryptographic method usually applied in online cloud environments that enables a system to provide an encrypted result without decrypting the processed private data (e.g. Munjal and Bhatia 2022).

1.4.2 Exercises: Can You Explain? (Check Yourself)

1. What does "usable" privacy and information security conceptually mean?
2. On what assumption is research based in this area?
3. Why do software developers and designers need to be sensitised to consider the reasons for security flaws in the interaction between humans and computer systems?
4. List the five major privacy pitfalls faced by designers and the strategies to counter them.
5. What do the terms PETs and TETs mean?

Glossary

Heuristics Heuristics are the application of general short rules in situations of uncertainty and challenges of data protection or IT security.

Usability "Usability is a measure of how well a specific user in a specific context can use a product/design to achieve a defined goal effectively, efficiently, and satisfactorily" – Interaction Design Foundation (https://www.interaction-design. org/literature/topics/usability (accessed 8 Mar 2023)).

Usable Security and Privacy by Design "Usable security" and "privacy by design" refer to those methods and procedures in the development of software and technical products that place the user at the centre of the development of security and privacy components (s. Schmitt et al. 2017).

User Experience "The first requirement for an exemplary user experience is to meet the exact needs of the customer, without fuss or bother. Next comes simplicity and elegance that produce products that are a joy to own, a joy to use. True user experience goes far beyond giving customers what they say they want, or providing checklist features. In order to achieve high-quality user experience in a company's offerings there must be a seamless merging of the services of multiple disciplines, including engineering, marketing, graphical and industrial design, and interface design" (https://www.nngroup.com/articles/definition-user-experience/ (accessed 8 Mar 2023)).

Further Reading

Cranor LF, Garfinkel S (eds) (2005) Security and usability: designing secure systems that people can use. O'Reilly, Beijing; Sebastapol, CA

Reuter C, Iacono L, Benlian A (2022) A quarter century of usable security and privacy research: transparency, tailorability, and the road ahead. Behav Inform Technol 41(10):2035–2048

Whitten A, Tygar JD (1999) Why Johnny can't encrypt: a usability evaluation of PGP 5.0. In: Proceedings of the 8th USENIX security symposium, 23–26 Aug 1999, Washington, DC, pp 169–184

References

Acquisti A (2004) Privacy and security of personal information. In: Economics of information security. Springer, Boston, MA, pp 179–186

Acquisti A (2009) Nudging privacy: the behavioral economics of personal information. IEEE Secur Priv 7(6):82–85

Acquisti A, Adjerid I, Balebako R et al (2017) Nudges for privacy and security: understanding and assisting users' choices online. ACM Comput Surveys 50(3):4

Adams A, Sasse AM (1999) Users are not the enemy. Commun ACM 42(12):40–46

Almuhimedi H, Schaub F, Sadeh N et al. (2015) Your location has been shared 5,398 times! A field study on mobile app privacy nudging. In: Proceedings of the conference on human factors in computing systems (CHI'15). ACM, pp 1–10

Beck H (2014) Behavioral economics. Eine Einführung. Springer Gabler, Wiesbaden

Bertino E (2020) Privacy in the era of 5G, IoT, big data and machine learning. In: 2020 Second IEEE international conference on trust, privacy and security in intelligent systems and applications (TPS-ISA). IEEE, pp 134–137

Brüggemann T, Hansen J, Dehling T et al (2016) An information privacy risk index for mHealth apps. In: Annual privacy forum. Springer, Cham, pp 190–201

Chiasson S, Forget A, Biddle R, van Oorschot PC (2008) Influencing users towards better passwords: persuasive cued click-points. In: Proceedings of the 22nd British HCI group annual conference on people and computers. British Computer Society, Swinton, UK, pp 121–130

Cranor LF (2008) A framework for reasoning about the human in the loop. https://www.usenix.org/legacy/event/upsec/tech/full_papers/cranor/cranor.pdf. Accessed 3 Mar 2023

Cranor LF, Garfinkel S (eds) (2005) Security and usability: designing secure systems that people can use. O'Reilly, Beijing; Sebastapol, CA

Dinev T, Hart P (2006) An extended privacy calculus model for e-commerce transactions. Inf Syst Res 17:61–80. https://doi.org/10.1287/isre.1060.0080

Dykstra J (2020) Invisible security: protecting users with no time to spare. In: 2020 IEEE 6th international conference on collaboration and internet computing (CIC)

Fuhrberg R (2019) Verhaltensökonomie in der Verwaltungskommunikation–Der Staat als Entscheidungsarchitekt. In: Öffentliche Verwaltung–Verwaltung in der Öffentlichkeit. Springer VS, Wiesbaden, pp 77–101

Garfinkel S (2005) Design principles and patterns for computer systems that are simultaneously secure and usable. Doctoral Thesis (Massachusetts Institute of Technology – MIT). https://dspace.mit.edu/handle/1721.1/33204. Accessed 3 Nov 2022

Gigerenzer G (2015) On the supposed evidence for libertarian paternalism. Rev Philos Psychol 6(3):361–383

Kahneman D (2012) Schnelles denken, langsames Denken. Siedler Verlag, Munich

Kerckhoffs A (1883 Jan) La Cryptographie Militaire. Journal des sciences militaires IX: 5–38. Cited in Reuter et al. (2022: 2)

Kirlappos I, Sasse MA (2014) What usable security really means: trusting and engaging users. In: International conference on human aspects of information security, privacy, and trust. Springer, Cham, pp 69–78

Lederer S, Hong J, Dey A et al (2004) Personal privacy through understanding and action: five pitfalls for designers. Carnegie Mellon University, Pittsburgh, PA

McDonald AM, Cranor LF (2008) The cost of reading privacy policies. I/S 4(3):543–568

Mills S (2022) Personalized nudging. Behav Public Policy 6(1):150–159

Munjal K, Bhatia R (2022) A systematic review of homomorphic encryption and its contributions in healthcare industry. Complex Intell Syst. https://doi.org/10.1007/s40747-022-00756-z

OECD (2017) Use of behavioural insights in consumer policy. In: OECD science, technology and industry policy papers, No. 36. OECD, Paris

Park YJ (2013) Digital literacy and privacy behavior online. Comm Res 40(2):215–236

Petitcolas F (2011) Kerckhoffs principle. In: van Tilborg HCA, Jajodia S (eds) Encyclopedia of cryptography and security, 2nd edn. Springer, Berlin

Reuter C, Iacono L, Benlian A (2022) A quarter century of usable security and privacy research: transparency, tailorability, and the road ahead. Behav Inform Technol 41(10):2035–2048

Ritter FE, Baxter GD, Churchill EF (2014) Foundations for designing user-centered systems. Springer, London

Sasse MA, Smith M, Herley C et al (2016) Debunking security-usability tradeoff myths. IEEE Secur Privacy 14(5):33–39. https://doi.org/10.1109/MSP.2016.110

Schaub F, Cranor LF (2020) Usable and useful privacy interfaces. In: Breaux TD (ed) An introduction to privacy for technology professionals. IAPP, Portsmouth, NH

Schmitt H, Nehren P, Lo Iacono L, Gorski PL (2017) Usable security and privacy by design. Software & Support Media, Frankfurt

Sunstein C (2016) The ethics of influence: government in the age of behavioral science. Cambridge University Press, Cambridge

Sunyaev A, Dehling T, Taylor PL et al (2015) Availability and quality of mobile health app privacy policies. J Am Med Inf Assoc 22(e1):e28–e33

Tavani H (2007) Philosophical theories of privacy: implications for an adequate online privacy policy. Metaphilosophy 38:1–22. https://doi.org/10.1111/j.1467-9973.2006.00474.x

Tavani H, Moor J (2001) Privacy protection, control of information, and privacy-enhancing technologies. ACM Sigcas Comput Soc 31:6–11. https://doi.org/10.1145/572277.572278

Thaler RH, Sunstein CR (2008) Nudge. Improving decisions about health, wealth, and happiness. Yale University Press, New Haven, CT

Thaler RH, Sunstein CR (2011) Nudge. Wie man kluge Entscheidungen anstößt. Ullstein, Berlin

Thorun C, Cerulli-Harms A, Micklitz HW, et al (2021) Nudge 2.0: Neue Anwendungen verhaltenswissenschaftlicher Erkenntnisse in der Verbraucherpolitik. Eine Vorstudie im Auftrag des Ministeriums für Ländlichen Raum und Verbraucherschutz (MLR) Baden-Württemberg, Stuttgart. Friedrichshafen: Forschungszentrum Verbraucher, Markt und Politik I CCMP (Hrsg.). 2. Auflage

Tversky A, Kahneman D (1981) The framing of decisions and the psychology of choice. Science 211(4481):453–458

van den Hoven J, Blaauw M, Pieters W et al (2016) Privacy and information technology. In: Zalta EN (ed) The Stanford encyclopedia of philosophy, Spring 2016 edn. https://plato.stanford.edu/entries/it-privacy/

Wang Y, Leon PG, Acquisti A et al (2014) A field trial of privacy nudges for Facebook. In: Proceedings of the 32nd annual ACM conference on human factors in computing systems (CHI'14). ACM, New York, NY, pp 2367–2376

Whitten A (2004) Making security usable. PhD thesis, School of Computer Science, Carnegie Mellon University

Whitten A, Tygar JD (1999) Why Johnny can't encrypt: a usability evaluation of PGP 5.0. In: Proceedings of the 8th USENIX security symposium, 23–26 Aug 1999, Washington, DC, pp 169–184

Xu H, Teo HH, Tan BC et al (2012) Research Note—Effects of individual self-protection, industry self-regulation, and government regulation on privacy concerns: a study of location-based services. Inf Sys Res 23(4):1342–1363

Zhao C, Zhao S, Zhao M et al (2019) Secure multi-party computation: theory, practice and applications. Inf Sci 476:357–372

Zimmermann C (2015) A categorization of transparency-enhancing technologies. https://www.researchgate.net/publication/280221171_A_Categorization_of_Transparency-Enhancing_Technologies. Accessed 27 Nov 2022

Chapter 2
Usability in Online Public Services

This chapter concentrates on the specific usability features of online public services situated in the context of the electronic government (e-government). Usability is a core aspect of the online public services development process. It seeks to satisfy citizens' and public servants' needs and necessities but also to improve and enhance the privacy and security of the whole online public system. Usability relies on several methods to support designers, analysts and online public services users (citizens and public servants interacting in the context of e-government). Usability methods first help to identify the system requirements and further to confirm that the system meets those requirements under the basic criteria of efficiency, effectiveness, safety, utility, ease of learning, ease of remembering, ease of using and evaluating, practical visibility and usage satisfaction. In the specific context of e-government and more concretely in the development and implementation of online public services, these usability criteria should serve to confirm that online public services support citizens' digital sovereignty in terms of citizens' confidence in controlling, using and understanding digital facilities (BMWi 2021: 9). For designers of online public services, this means the need to include these usability criteria in their development agenda to enhance technology acceptance and performance and satisfy citizens' needs as well as those of public servants working in the delivery of public services.

2.1 Online Public Services in the Framework of E-Government and the Importance of Usability

The provision of public services is one of the main tasks of governments (Meijer and Bekkers 2015; Meijer et al. 2018). During the last two decades, governments have used information and telecommunication (IT) facilities to provide their services to citizens. As a result of the usage of these IT facilities, including telecommunication

Table 2.1 E-government relations and public services (based on Kubicek et al. 2011: 2)

E-government relation	Examples of public services
G2C/C2G	Tax declarations, applications for social benefits, requests for birth certificates or driver's licenses, etc.
G2B/B2G	Social contributions for employees, declarations of corporate tax, and different kinds of permits for export, environmental emissions, etc.
G2G	Access to central registries by local authorities, sharing of information resources.

infrastructures, some public services have evolved to online public services (OPS), which in general terms are those services provided by governments through digital technologies on the internet. These OPS are framed in specific electronic government (e-government) structures that comprise several relations between the government and the public supported by IT means. E-government includes the relations between citizens (C) and governments (G) (C2G and G2C) and business (B) and governments (B2G and G2B) and those internal relations between different organisations within the government system (G2G) taking place on the internet or supported by IT means.[1] Kubicek et al. (2011) give some examples of the public services that correspond to each of these e-government relations (see Table 2.1). Users of OPS in the framework of e-government are citizens, businesses and public administrations accessing and using public services online.[2]

Well-functioning communication is a requisite for the good quality of G2C and G2B relations. To understand the communication embedded in these relations, it is necessary to distinguish between back-office and front-office agencies. Whenever citizens or business applies for a public service in a front-office agency on the internet, back-office agencies interact to supply and activate the necessary documents, protocols and procedures. The interoperability between the agencies' systems is crucial for a successful process. An example of this is citizens' registration when they move their residence to another community location (Kubicek et al. 2011). In Germany, because of federalism, citizens' registration was decentralised. Many different software systems operated in local civil registries. Citizens had to deregister in their former community location to be able to register in their new one—this is why the same data had to be redundantly provided for this task in two different locations. To avoid bureaucratic burdens of redundant data delivery and improve data validity, the law was changed. A data exchange format and an interface were mandatorily established by law (Kubicek et al. 2011: 5). The development of an interoperable system based on a common data exchange format made it possible for

---

[1] See von Lücke and Reinmann (2002) for a detailed explanation of the e-government relations.

[2] See for the EU case principle 6 "user centricity" of the EU OPS in the European Interoperability Framework (EIF): https://joinup.ec.europa.eu/collection/nifo-national-interoperability-framework-observatory/2-underlying-principles-european-public-services#2.7. Accessed 15 Dec 2022.

only interfaces to be added to the many different local systems operating in back-office agencies.

From a supranational perspective, the G2G e-government level is particularly complex. For example, in the framework of the European Interoperability Framework (EIF) of the European Union (EU), we can distinguish e-government G2G interoperability relationships, including relationships such as those between EU member states' administrations or between administrative institutions of EU member states.

In the framework of these relationships, OPS are those government services defined and legitimised as public and thus legally supported and protected within the specific (national, supranational) government structures (partially) established on the internet. Partially means here that online access is not necessarily the only channel to access public services. The inclusion and accessibility principle of the EIF, for example, supports the multichannel coexistence of analogue and digital public services provision. Thus, the provision of OPS is not just a technological endeavour. The digitalisation process of OPS and the implementation of digital system interoperability are related to the political e-government ideas of the socio-cultural contexts in which they are developed and implemented (Kubicek et al. 2011).

E-government relationships as well as the implementation of OPS on the internet are dynamic processes affected by several social, legal and economic events (i.e. the COVID-19 pandemic) and by the transformation of political programmes and governance priorities. The political e-government ideas of using IT for the transformation of the public sector towards a more effective and efficient provision of public services have been related to the reform ideas of the so-called New Public Management (NPM) (Cordella and Bonina 2012). The use of IT in the public sector, as Cordella and Bonina (2012) explain, has been driven by NPM reform goals of making the public sector administration more efficient, streamlined, downsized and consistent in line with objectives that are usual in market economics. These authors also point out that the ideas underlying these objectives are in contrast to traditional assumptions of bureaucratic efficiency and democracy of delivering public services following the principles of impersonality, equality and fairness (Cordella and Bonina 2012: 513). Managerial values driving NPM have replaced these bureaucratic and democracy assumptions in e-government, including OPS provision. However, managerial values rooted in the private sector are not completely suitable for the public sector since their targets radically differ from each other. The private sector seeks to create private benefits, whereas the public sector's target is to create public value for citizens achieving government programmes' objectives and delivering public services. Thus, prioritising public value creation in the deployment of IT in the public sector also means using IT to improve governance and enhance democratic processes (Cordella and Bonina 2012). From this public value perspective, e-government development and the implementation of OPS are means to establish public trust and participatory relations between the government and citizens but also to guarantee digital sovereignty[3] (see Chap. 4).

Usability of the OPS or synonymously "user centricity" is thus considered necessary to achieve public values in e-government. As Inglesant and Sasse (2007) emphasise, usability is crucial in the development of e-government because of the importance of good public services as public value sources that strengthen political legitimacy. Second, governments pursue wide policy outcomes such as social inclusion, environmental sustainability and community well-being with the provision of public services. Therefore, the usability evaluation of public services should consider these wider outcomes of public services implementation. However, usability is overlooked in e-government development. Moreover, as Inglesant and Sasse (2007) explain, commonly applied usability definitions following the ISO 9241 Part 11 standard are too restrictively concentrated on efficiency, effectiveness and satisfaction. This usability standard ignores that usability is not only about software for office work. Usability for e-government also includes users' intentional and emotional reasons to use online services, which can be considered intrinsic motivation based on interest and enjoyment in using the system (Inglesant and Sasse 2007). In the context of e-government and OPS, trust and transparency are crucial usability aspects that enhance users' adoption and motivation.

In the practice of the development and implementation of OPS, usability should help to identify system requirements to create public value and achieve digital sovereignty for every citizen. We will explain in detail the concept of digital sovereignty in Chap. 4. Furthermore, usability methods for OPS should support the confirmation of meeting those requirements according to the basic criteria of efficiency, effectiveness, safety, utility, ease of learning, ease of remembering, ease of using and evaluating, practical visibility and usage satisfaction. Related to these aspects, it is also important to consider how to build trust in e-government relationships and in the usage of privacy and security measures in OPS.

In sum, due to their public nature, OPS must be available and accessible for every citizen, and while using them, data privacy and information security must be guaranteed. Thus, usability aspects such as the legal correctness and understanding of the terminology used, the ease of services and data privacy rule findability are necessary features in the design of OPS. These features are linked to the concepts of privacy and security by design and by default, which we will explain in Chap. 4.

Necessary for the implementation of usable secure OPS are the interoperability of the OPS system and a secure user identification process to access and use the OPS. In the next section, we explain the concept of interoperability and how it is connected to usability.

---

[3]For a detailed explanation of "digital sovereignty", see, i.e. Floridi (2020). Goldacker (2017) emphasises that digital sovereignty should be considered from multiple perspectives including data sovereignty, cybersecurity, competency over core digital technologies as well as the successful usage of IT (Goldacker 2017: 5).

2.2   Interoperability of OPS and the Role of Usability

Interoperability has been defined in various ways in the past, mostly referring to technological features (Kubicek et al. 2011; Campmas et al. 2022). Pardo et al. (2012: 8) define interoperability from a sociotechnical perspective as a "set of multidimensional, complementary, and dynamic capabilities that are specific to a defined network of organizations with particular goals and a common environment" and emphasise the importance of this concept in the context of e-government as a central capability for a connected government. In the context of the EU e-government, the ETSI (2022: 4) definition serves as a contextual reference: "the ability of two or more systems or applications to exchange information and to mutually use the information that has been exchanged". As a part of the European Interoperability Strategy (EIS), the European Interoperability Reference Architecture (EIRA) has been created and endorsed by the European Commission in its European Interoperability Framework (EIF), which is based upon 12 EU OPS principles and comprises 6 interconnected layers: technological, sematic, organisational, legal, integrated public service governance and interoperability governance.[4]

One of the 12 EU OPS principles explicitly related to usability is "user centricity". This principle includes the following expectations for the development of the EU OPS: a multichannel service delivery approach (availability of alternative channels, physical and digital to access OPS), single point of contact (SPOC),[5] systematic collection of users' feedback to improve the OPS, once-only principle (OOP) of data and the limitation of requested information for OPS usage to the necessary.

The interoperability of OPS systems should support correct OPS usage and management across multiple government levels and a good user experience. Interoperability is related not only to technical standards and interfaces but also to organisational, social and cultural aspects (Kubicek et al. 2011; Campmas et al. 2022). At the G2G relationship level of e-government, interoperability requires sociopolitical, economic and cultural intergovernmental cooperation. The internal workflows between the multiple organisations involved in OPS provision and the software systems they use must be adapted to successfully accomplish joint OPS delivery to citizens and businesses. A common language for understanding, communication and data exchange must also be established. Therefore, one important step to achieve interoperability or, more concretely, semantic interoperability—one

---

[4] https://joinup.ec.europa.eu/collection/nifo-national-interoperability-framework-observatory/european-interoperability-framework-detail. Accessed 15 Dec 2022.

[5] https://ec.europa.eu/digital-building-blocks/wikis/display/DIGITAL/Find+your+Single+Point+of+Contact. Accessed 16 Dec 2022.

of the six layers of the EIF—is the development of ontologies[6] and taxonomies[7] of OPS, which need a consensus among the involved stakeholders to be standardised and implemented.

For example, in the case of the EU's Single Digital Gateway (SDG),[8] the experts of the European Commission's Programme ISA2 (ISA2 2019) have elaborated a taxonomy of generic public services in the European Union (EU) to help EU member states' public administrations harmonise their catalogue of online public services or, in other words, to enable their interoperability. In the case of multinational OPS, a standardised taxonomy provides service content structure and organisation as well as a reference and authoritative source of content assets for content management systems on which the e-government stakeholders involved in the design, development and implementation of online public services across the EU can rely. From the usability point of view, a taxonomy relates specific finding architectures[9] and supports a consistent user experience across related platforms. An example of this taxonomy in the delivery of online public services in the EU is the Finnish OPS portal in Fig. 2.1.

The taxonomy of the Finnish OPS portal shown in Fig. 2.1 combines two perspectives: the user perspective (i.e. information and services for citizens) and general topics (i.e. social security) (ISA2 2019).

The Finnish OPS portal is just one national case of EU e-government. Today, in 2023, the OPS portals will very much differ between the 27 EU member states. A European Interoperability Cartography (EIC)[10] offers an overview of the different interoperability solutions existing in the EU.

Looking towards the mandatory implementation of the single digital gateway regulation[11] until the end of 2023, a general taxonomy has been implemented for the EU OPS portal "Your Europe".[12] This taxonomy helps to structure services in a stable, nonredundant and consistent way. It corresponds to the single digital gateway regulation that includes three strategic targets: first, the reduction of administrative burdens of citizens and business in the exercise of their EU rights; second, the

---

[6] See https://joinup.ec.europa.eu/collection/eprocurement/solution/eprocurement-ontology (accessed 16 Dec 2022).

[7] A taxonomy can be understood as a controlled vocabulary, which means an authoritative list of terms used in indexing with a hierarchical structure (ISA2 2019). For a detailed explanation of previous taxonomies in the framework of EU e-government, see Kubicek et al. (2011).

[8] The SDG accessible through a search function in the "Your Europe" digital portal aims to facilitate online information, administrative procedures and assistance services to citizens and businesses across the EU [https://single-market-economy.ec.europa.eu/single-market/single-digital-gateway_ en (accessed 16 Dec 2022)].

[9] This refers to the way in which the terms are classified and related to be found in specific queries.

[10] https://joinup.ec.europa.eu/collection/cartography/solution/european-interoperability-cartogra phy-eic. Accessed 16 Dec 2022.

[11] https://eur-lex.europa.eu/legal-content/EN/TXT/?uri=uriserv:OJ.L_.2018.295.01.0001.01.ENG. Accessed 13 Dec 2022.

[12] https://europa.eu/youreurope/citizens/index_en.htm. Accessed 13 Dec 2022.

Fig. 2.1 Taxonomy of OPS in Finland. Source: https://www.suomi.fi/citizen. Accessed 15 Jul 2023

elimination of discrimination; and third, "the functioning of the internal market with regard to the provision of information, of procedures and of assistance and problem-solving services".[13] These targets fit the three main pillars of the EU single digital market, of which the single digital gateway is a part. Since access to OPS constitutes a main usability target, these three pillars[14] are directly related to the usability of the OPS.

Access to public services is not a unilateral task in the provision of OPS. The e-government relation between governments and citizens (G2C/C2G) also involves citizens' active agency to communicate with governments or to register into OPS portals to use the provided OPS. From a data privacy perspective, both actors, the

---

[13] https://eur-lex.europa.eu/legal-content/EN/TXT/?uri=uriserv:OJ.L_.2018.295.01.0001.01. ENG&toc=OJ:L:2018:295:TOC. Accessed 13 Dec 2022.

[14] Access to digital goods and services; environment, which refers to the appropriate conditions for flourishing digital networks and services; and economy and society, which refers to the maximisation of the growth potential of the digital economy (ISA2 2019).

Table 2.2 Principles of web accessibility in WCAG 2.1 from W3C https://www.w3.org/TR/WCAG21/#new-features-in-wcag-2-1. Accessed 10 Dec 2022

WCAG 2.1 principles	Definition and guidelines
Perceivable	Information and user interface components must be presentable to users in ways they can perceive. (Guidelines: Text alternatives, Time-based media, adaptable, distinguishable).
Operable	User interface components and navigation must be operable. (Guidelines: Keyboard accessible, enough time, seizures, and physical reactions, navigable, input modalities).
Understandable	Information and the operation of user interface must be understandable. (Guidelines: Readable, predictable, input assistance).
Robustness	Content must be robust enough that it can be interpreted by a wide variety of user agents, including assistive technologies. (Guidelines: Compatible).

government (in an extended sense, the government administrations and private organisations enabling the usage of OPS) and citizens, share the responsibility of data security in the usage of OPS in an asymmetric way (see Chap. 1). For example, when citizens register to access OPS using their email credentials and a self-chosen password, they should be aware of the data privacy and security risks implied in this task. For that, citizens need specific understandable information and certain digital skills (see Chap. 3).

This C2G interaction relates to two other important aspects of OPS usability: the OPS design accomplishment to the Web Accessibility Directive (WAD)[15] and to the understanding of data privacy and information security in the identification and authentication procedures to access OPS by all citizens. The WAD that entered into force on 22 December 2016 requires websites and mobile applications of public sector bodies (PSBs) to meet accessibility requirements based on the Harmonised European Standard EN 301 549 V2.1.2 (2018-08) and on the WCAG 2.1 from W3C.[16] The WAD covers the accessibility of textual and nontextual information, downloadable documents and forms as well as processing of digital forms and completing authentication, identification and payment transactions.

Four basic principles guide the WAD based on WCAG 2.1 from W3C, as we show in Table 2.2. To support the implementation of the WAD, the EU-funded project WADcher has developed a unified web accessibility assessment framework (Spyrou et al. 2019). Moreover, the quick reference guide provided by W3C helps to provide an overview of the web accessibility principles and guidelines during the implementation of usability testing. From a usable privacy and security perspective,

---

[15] https://digital-strategy.ec.europa.eu/en/policies/web-accessibility. Accessed 16 Dec 2022.

[16] A quick reference guide of this standard can be found in https://www.w3.org/WAI/WCAG21/quickref/ (accessed 16 Dec 2022).

W3C is the World Wide Web Consortium funded in 1994 by Tim Berners-Lee dedicated to the technical specifications and guidelines of the World Wide Web.

See https://www.seo-analyse.com/seo-lexikon/w/w3c/ (accessed 24 Feb 2023).

we suggest adding these principles and guidelines to the aspects of data privacy and security. This means, for example, answering the questions of whether data privacy and security protocols in OPS are perceivable, operable, understandable and robust.

With respect to the accomplishment to the WAD, each EU member state is required every 3 years to report on the results of their monitoring activities. A study (European Commission 2022) covering the first 3 years of review of the WAB application in public sector bodies reveals several implementation shortcomings (insufficient accessibility expertise, that some member states do not involve end-users in the testing phase, that some key elements are optional and rarely reported on (e.g. accessibility statements, feedback mechanisms and use of the disproportionate burden clause), lack of awareness of the minimum requirements, etc.). To improve the interoperability of OPS in the EU, the Commission has adopted the Interoperable Europe Act (IEA) in 2022 to strengthen the cooperation between public administrations. The IEA, steered by the Interoperable Europe Board (IEB), introduces a structured EU cooperation and mandatory assessments to evaluate the impact of IT systems transformations for EU interoperability, sharing and reuse solutions integrated in an interoperable Europe portal as well as innovation and support measures.[17] These measures will also support the governance of OPS accessibility and usage in the EU.

2.3   E-Identity for OPS Usage and Usability

In the framework of e-government, governments require citizens and businesses to prove their identities or specific attributes (for authentication and authorisation) to demonstrate eligibility for OPS. Electronic identity (e-identity) enables this proof to access OPS. E-identity is not the same as a digital identity card, but in some cases, both can overlap. While the e-identity or eID is a means to prove the identity of a citizen, business or administration in the framework of e-government considering that those three entities may have different parallel roles in multiple sectors (i.e. a civil servant, a mother, a tax payer, etc.), a digital identity is rather a replacement of national identity cards with digital functions proving that the person is a citizen of a specific country. Depending on the decisions in the specific country and its legislation, the digital identity card (the physical token containing the digital identity proof) can also be a container for identity proof in other identity roles[18] related to OPS. Thus, for example, in the EU, the use of the digital card as an e-identity differs among the member states. Moreover, there might exist several documents providing

---

[17] https://ec.europa.eu/commission/presscorner/detail/en/ip_22_6907. Accessed 3 Jan 2023.

[18] See https://ec.europa.eu/information_society/activities/ict_psp/documents/eid_introduction.pdf (accessed 19 Dec 2022).

the personal data of the holder. In Germany,[19] examples of these multiple documents include electronic ID cards, electronic passports and electronic residence permits, which have an incorporated chip.

From a multinational perspective, in the EU, digital eID is a set of services (software, documentation, training and support) that the European Commission provides to support the public administrations and private service providers of the member states in their mutual recognition of national electronic identification (eID) schemes (including smartcards, mobile and log-in).[20] Since 2018, the obligatory mutual recognition of electronic identities in the EU has been based on the eIDAS regulation[21] mandate. The mutually recognised eID is crucial to implement the EIF once-only principle (OOP), which aims to improve the usability of OPS, avoiding redundant citizens' and businesses' data provision in their interaction with governments while encouraging national governments to internally share and reuse the data already provided.

In Article 8, the eIDAS regulation introduced three levels of assurance for electronic identification (low, substantial and high), which enable access to different OPS depending on the sensitivity degree of the information accessible after the authentication procedure.[22] The high assurance level using eID for identification enables access to all available OPS, whereas substantial (at least two-factor identification) and low (authentication with username and password) assurance levels allow access to a more restricted number of OPS.

Moreover, eIDAS regulation has introduced the concept of Qualified Trust Service Providers (QTSP) that are supervised accredited service providers to perform so-called trusted services such as issuing signatures certificates, signatures validation, timestamping, etc. QTSP must follow European Telecommunications Standards Institute's (ETSI) standards and need an accreditation of the conformity assessment body and the approval of the national supervisory body.[23] Trust services are particularly supportive in the framework of the EU single market for business-to-consumer transactions, for example, in the financial service sector.

Table 2.3 shows the electronic identification and the five core trust services already in use for EU citizens and business.[24]

For citizens, business and public organisations, an important function of eID is access to OPS using digital accounts. These digital accounts facilitate the

---

[19] https://www.bsi.bund.de/EN/Themen/Oeffentliche-Verwaltung/Elektronische-Identitaeten/elektronische-identitaeten_node.html. Accessed 19 Dec 2022.

[20] https://ec.europa.eu/digital-building-blocks/wikis/display/DIGITAL/What+is+eID.   Accessed 19 Dec 2022.

[21] https://digital-strategy.ec.europa.eu/en/policies/eidas-regulation. Accessed 20 Dec 2022.

[22] https://ec.europa.eu/digital-building-blocks/wikis/display/DIGITAL/eIDAS+Levels+of+Assur ance. Accessed 20 Dec 2022.

[23] https://fidoalliance.org/wp-content/uploads/2020/04/FIDO-deploying-FIDO2-eIDAS-QTSPs-eID-schemes-white-paper.pdf. Accessed 20 Dec 2022.

[24] https://commission.europa.eu/strategy-and-policy/priorities-2019-2024/europe-fit-digital-age/european-digital-identity_en. Accessed 5 Jan 2023.

Table 2.3 Identification and trust services in use for EU citizens and business

Electronic identification (eID) and trust services	Functions
eID	Proves citizens' and business identity electronically
eSignature	Expression of a person's agreement to the content of a document in electronic form
eTimestamp	Electronic proof that data exist at a specific time
eSeal	Guarantees the origin and integrity of a document
Qualified Website Authentication Certificate	Ensures that websites are trustworthy and reliable
Electronic Registered Delivery Service	Protection against the risk of loss, theft, damage or alteration when sending documentations

implementation of the OOP principle. Citizens, business and public organisations can register in these accounts just once and use their registered identification whenever they need to access OPS. For example, in Germany, in the framework of the Online Access Act (OAA),[25] citizens can register in digital accounts to access OPS at different levels of assurance.

The German federal registration page coexists with the pages offered by the federal states. In our research project Instruments for active and safe consumer participation on Online Public Services (IVTOPS), we explore user adoption of these pages. The results of our research reveal that citizens confront several usable privacy and security problems using these accounts, such as difficulties finding the data privacy statements, redundancies in the registration buttons or finding explanations about the levels of assurance. Moreover, users participating in our research do not notice the once-only function of the user accounts.

From a usable privacy and security perspective, it is important to consider the awareness and user centricity of the identification and authentication solutions to access OPS. For example, in the framework of the EU, an evaluation of the eIDAS implementation in the member states (European Commission 2018) has revealed that some of the most important shortcomings are the lack of awareness of eIDs and the usability failures of the user interfaces and fragmented visual identities, which decrease users' trust in the authenticity of the transaction processes.

The usability evaluation of the European Commission (2018) covers four phases of eIDAS usage: applying, understanding and discovering, using and managing. With respect to applying, related to obtaining an eID, the study found that the application process can be confusing and difficult. Moreover, there is a lack of eID onboarding. Regarding the understanding and discovery of eIDAS, for citizens, the concept of an eID remains difficult to understand. Furthermore, the interface design may lead users to not use the cross-border authentication option. Additionally, during the use of an eID, users confront several usability obstacles: the length and

---

[25] https://www.onlinezugangsgesetz.de/Webs/OZG/EN/home/home-node.html.   Accessed 21 Dec 2022.

disjointed nature of the authentication procedure, the unintuitive means of selecting their preferred eID scheme and the lack of information about the different options to make an informed choice. The attribute consent during the authentication procedure is also unintuitive and time-consuming. The user journey is inconsistent and can lead users to mistrust the handling of their personal data.

Another usability shortcoming in the use phase of an eID is that even if users may be able to log in to a service, they may not be eligible to use it. Users may also experience the inability to authenticate when they are abroad in the same way as when they are at home. Moreover, they may confront difficulties in the identification processes due to data mismatches between member states. Regarding the fourth phase of data management, usability failures refer to the difficulties of obtaining an eID or changing its attributes (such as vaccination passports, driving licence, professional qualification, etc.) while users are in another EU member state or for renewal due to the requirement of physical presence in the country of issuance (European Commission 2018). Moreover, not all countries in the EU have established the same procedures of digital citizens' identity authentication.[26] For example, in Estonia, citizens and business can identify through a centralised data exchange platform and unique personal identifiers (UPI), whereas in Germany, there is not a consistent UPI approach, and different data exchange platforms coexist (Shehu et al. 2019).

As a result of the eIDAS evaluation and disappointing findings regarding the poor use and usability of eID in the EU, the regulatory eIDAS framework has been revised, including 139 amendments in 2021 (Tenhunen 2022). A part of these eIDAS amendments introduces the EU Digital Identity Wallet (EUDI Wallet)[27] to ensure trustworthy digital transactions such as signing, preservation and archiving, identification, sharing attributes and authentication.

The EUDI Wallet should enable EU citizens access to trusted digital identity provided by their respective national governments and accepted by the EU member states as well as by the European Free Trade Association (EFTA). The EUDI Wallet will also enable the collection of additional personal data (i.e. educational certificates) that can be used for private as well as for public service transactions. Thus, the EUDI Wallet will be integrated into an ecosystem of supporting organisations issuing attributes and facilitating the sharing of credentials. The consideration of establishing EUDI Wallet responds not only to deficits in the usage of centralised identity eID solutions, including usability failures, but also to the increasing relevance of the digital attributes that citizens are obliged to use in rapidly digitalising societies. In this digitalisation process, the amount of identity-sensitive and personalised services for an increasing number of diversified use cases has grown substantially. The exchange of attributes related to digital identities has become even

---

[26] https://ec.europa.eu/digital-building-blocks/wikis/display/DIGITAL/Country+overview. Accessed 11 Jan 2023.

[27] See the outline of the 2022 European Digital Identity Architecture and Reference Framework in https://ec.europe.eu/newsroom/dae/redirection/document83643 (accessed 9 Jan 2023).

Table 2.4 SSI principles (see Allen 2016)

SSI principles	Explanation
Existence	Independent existence of the users. The SSI makes public and accessible limited aspects of the existing "I"
Control	Control of identities by the users. The ultimate authority of their identities are the users
Consent	Sharing of users' identity data needs the consent of the users
Access	Access to the users' own data
Transparency	The system to administer and operate a network of identities must be open. The algorithms should be free, open-source, well-known and as independent as possible
Portability	Information and services about identities must be transportable. Identities must not be held by a singular third-party entity to ensure that the users maintain the control over their identities over time
Interoperability	The use of the identities must be as widely as possible
Persistence	The identities should last as long as the users wish
Minimalisation	In case of identity data disclosure, this disclosure should involve only the minimum amount of data necessary for the requesting task
Protection	The rights of the users must be protected. Algorithms used for identity authentication must be independent, censorship-resistant and force-resilient and run in a decentralised manner

more important than the related digital identities of users. COVID-19 certificates are an example of this (Pöhn et al. 2021).

In any case, digital identity providers are today not exclusively national governments. For example, in the EU, the traditional digital identity solutions provided by national governments coexist with a highly fragmented and competitive private sector of digital identity services that includes telecommunication companies, finance services and banks or social media platforms (Busch 2022; ENISA 2022). A common framework for this fragmented digital identity market is the implementation of the so-called self-sovereign identities (SSI) concept.

The EUDI Wallet is based on the concept of SSI. Aiming to enable users to control their digital identities, Allen (2016) coined this concept with ten principles summarised in Table 2.4. Tobin and Reed (2016) grouped these principles into three categories: security (protection, persistence, minimisation), controllability (existence, control, consent) and portability (interoperability, transparency, access).

Basically, the SSI concept relies on the idea of decentralising the digital identity and attribute management of individuals in societies. The methods of identity and attribute management have evolved from the centralised, user-centred and federated methods towards the SSI paradigm, which has emerged over the past few years. In the centralised method, the users' identities are controlled by central actors such as administrators. This method involves, among other things, redundant storage of the data and the risk of abusive use. To overcome these risks, in the user-centred approach, the identity subjects manage themselves regarding the usage of and access to their identities and attributes. This approach also includes data privacy and security risks (i.e. identity attributes must repeatedly be verified for each individual service, and the data remain stored by the respective service provider) and usability problems (lack of user friendliness).[28]

The SSI method is conceptually based upon Allen's (2016) principles and technologically requires five components: (1) verifiable credentials (VCs), (2) roles (issuer, holder and verifier), (3) decentralised identifiers (DID), (4) digital wallets and (5) digital agents and hubs (Strücker et al. 2021; Kubach and Roßnagel 2021; Martínez Jurado et al. 2021). In the SSI concept, the identity subjects (users) hold the keys to their digital identities, and the actors involved in the SSI ecosystem can only communicate about the identity subjects after directly contacting the identity subjects.

A target of the EUDI Wallet is to promote trusted digital identities allowing EU citizens to control their online interactions and transactions. Several use cases have been considered to develop the EUDI Wallet. The eIDAS expert group[29] has selected a set of five first use-case areas (secured and trusted identification to access online public and private services, health, education, digital finance and mobility and driving licences). In February 2022, the EU Commission launched a tender to develop the EUDI Wallet.[30] Several large-scale pilot projects will concentrate on different use cases (travelling, payments, professional qualifications, etc.)[31] of the EUDI Wallet's implementation.

In Chap. 4, we will explain some of the challenges of the EUDI Wallet from a usable privacy and security perspective.

2.4 Summary

- E-government includes the relations between citizens (C) and governments (G) (C2G and G2C) and business (B) and governments (B2G and G2B) and those internal relations between different organisations within the government system (G2G) taking place on the internet or supported by IT means. The e-government relation between governments and citizens (G2C/C2G) involves citizens' active agency to communicate with governments or to register into OPS portals to use the provided OPS.
- Whenever citizens or business applies for a public service in a front-office agency on the internet, back-office agencies interact to supply and activate the necessary

---

[28] https://www.w3.org/TR/vc-data-model. Accessed 8 Mar 2023.

[29] https://ec.europa.eu/transparency/expert-groups-register/screen/expert-groups/consult?lang=en&do=groupDetail.groupDetail&groupID=3032. Accessed 9 Jan 2023.

[30] https://ec.europa.eu/info/funding-tenders/opportunities/portal/screen/opportunities/topic-details/digital-2022-deploy-02-electronic-id. Accessed 10 Jan 2023.

[31] Examples of the current (2023) projects are https://www.nobidconsortium.com/ (focused on payments), https://eudiwalletconsortium.org/ (focused on travelling) and https://www.dc4eu.eu/ (focused on educational credentials, professional qualifications and social security) (accessed 10 Jan 2023).

documents, protocols and procedures. The interoperability between the agencies' systems is crucial for a successful process.

- The digitalisation process of OPS and the implementation of interoperable digital systems are related to the political e-government ideas of the sociocultural contexts where they are developed and implemented.
- E-government development and the implementation of OPS include establishing public trust and participatory relations between the government and citizens but also guaranteeing digital sovereignty.
- In the practice of the development and implementation of OPS, usability should help to identify system requirements to create public value and achieve digital sovereignty for every citizen.
- Due to their public nature, OPSs must be available and accessible for every citizen, and while using them, data privacy and information security must be guaranteed. Thus, usability aspects such as the legal correctness and understanding of the terminology used, the ease of services and data privacy rule findability are necessary features in the design of OPS.
- The interoperability of OPS systems should support correct OPS usage and management across multiple government levels and a good user experience. One important step to achieve semantic interoperability is the development of ontologies and taxonomies of OPS, which need a consensus among the involved stakeholders to be standardised and implemented.
- From the usability point of view, a taxonomy relates specific IT architectures and supports a consistent user experience across related platforms.
- The e-government C2G interaction relates to two important aspects of OPS usability: the OPS design accomplishment for the Web Accessibility Directive (WAD)[32] and for the understanding of data privacy and information security in the identification and authentication procedures to access OPS by all citizens.
- A part of the 2021 eIDAS amendments introduces the EU Digital Identity Wallet (EUDI Wallet) to ensure trustworthy digital transactions such as signing, preservation and archiving, identification, sharing attributes and authentication. The EUDI Wallet is based on the concept of "self-sovereign identities" (SSI) aiming to enable users to control their digital identities (Allen 2016).

2.5 Examples and Exercises

2.5.1 Examples

Examples of the implementation of eID schemes and the status of the eIDAS-Node across the EU can be found in the following: https://ec.europa.eu/digital-building-blocks/wikis/display/DIGITAL/Country+overview (accessed 22 May 2023).

---

[32] https://digital-strategy.ec.europa.eu/en/policies/web-accessibility. Accessed 16 Dec 2022.

2.5.2 Exercises: Can You Explain? (Check Yourself)

1. What do usability methods help with?
2. What is the purpose of usability criteria, especially for online public services?
3. Why should the developers and designers of such services consider usability criteria?
4. List 10 principles to empower users to take control of their digital identities.

Glossary

Attribute "A feature, characteristic or quality of a natural or legal person or of an entity, in electronic form" (European Commission 2023: 7).

Authentication "Verifying the identity of a user, process, or device, often as a prerequisite to allowing access to resources in an information system" [https://csrc.nist.gov/glossary/term/authentication (accessed 8 Mar 2023)].

Decentralised Identifiers (DID) "DIDs are a new type of identifier that enables verifiable, decentralized digital identity" [https://www.w3.org/TR/did-core/ (accessed 11 Jan 2023)].

E-Identification (eID) "eID is a set of services provided by the European Commission to enable the mutual recognition of national electronic identification schemes (eID) across borders. It allows European citizens to use their national eIDs when accessing online services from other European countries" [https://ec.europa.eu/digital-building-blocks/wikis/display/DIGITAL/eID (accessed 8 Mar 2023)].

Electronic Attestation of Attributes (EAAs) "An attestation in electronic form that allows the authentication of attributes" (European Commission 2023: 7).

EUDI Wallet "It can be seen as a combination of several products and Trust Services that enables Users to securely request, obtain and store their information allowing them to access online services, present data about them and electronically sign or seal documents" (European Commission 2023: 7).

Personal Identifiable data (PID) "A set of data enabling the identity of a natural or legal person, or a natural person representing a legal person to be established" (European Commission 2023: 7).

Single Digital Gateway "The single digital gateway facilitates online access to information, administrative procedures, and assistance services that EU citizens and businesses may need in another EU country. Access to the gateway is via a search function in the Your Europe portal which has been providing EU and national information on the rights of citizens and businesses, as well as access to assistance services, since 2006". See https://single-market-economy.ec.europa.eu/single-market/single-digital-gateway_en (accessed 8 Mar 2023).

Self-Sovereign Identity (SSI) "Self-sovereign identity is the next step beyond user-centric identity and that means it begins at the same place: the user must be central to the administration of identity. That requires not just the interoperability of a user's identity across multiple locations, with the user's consent, but also true user control of that digital identity, creating user autonomy" (Allen 2016).

Further Reading

European Commission (2023) The European digital identity wallet architecture and reference framework. https://digital-strategy.ec.europa.eu/en/library/european-digital-identity-wallet-architecture-and-reference-framework. Accessed 8 Mar 2023

ISA2 (2019) European Taxonomy for public services. Directorate-General for Informatics Directorate B — Interoperability Solutions for public administrations, businesses and citizens Unit B6 — ISA2 Programme. https://ec.europa.eu/isa2/news/new-level-cooperation-isa-building-interoperable-europe_en/. Accessed 12 Dec 2022

Pöhn D, Grabatin M, Hommel W (2021) eID and self-sovereign identity usage: an overview. Electronics 10(22):2811

Tenhunen S (2022) Revision of the eIDAS Regulation. Findings on its implementation and application. European Parliamentary Research Service (EPRS). https://www.europarl.europa.eu/RegData/etudes/BRIE/2022/699491/EPRS_BRI(2022)699491_EN.pdf.   Accessed 6 Jan 2023

References

Allen C (2016) The path to self-sovereign identity. Life with Alacrity. https://www.lifewithalacrity.com/2016/04/the-path-to-self-soverereign-identity.html. Accessed 10 Jan 2023

Bannister F, Connolly R (2014) ICT, public values and transformative government: a framework and programme for research. Gov Inf Quart 31:119–128

BMWi (Bundesministerium für Wirtschaft und Energie) (2021) Digitale Souveränität Bestandsaufnahme und Handlungsfelder. BMWi and ZEW Mannheim.

Bonina CM, Cordella A (2009) Public sector reforms and the notion of 'public value': implications for e-government deployment. In: Proceedings of the 15th Americas Conference on Information Systems, 6th–9th August, San Francisco, CA

Busch C (2022) eIDAS 2.0: Digital identity services in the platform economy. Centre on Regulation in Europe (CERRE)

Campmas A, Iacob N, Simonelli F (2022) How can interoperability stimulate the use of digital public services? An analysis of national interoperability frameworks and e-Government in the European Union. Data & Policy 4:E19

Cordella A, Bonina CM (2012) A public value perspective for ICT enabled public sector reforms: a theoretical reflection. Gov Inf Q 29(4):512–520

ENISA (2022) Digital identity: leveraging the self-sovereign identity (SSI) concept to build trust. (January 2022)

eSSIF Lab. https://gitlab.grnet.gr/essif-lab. Accessed 11 Jan 2023

ETSI (2022) ETSI GR PDL 006 V1.1.1. Permissioned Distributed Ledger (PDL); Inter-Ledger interoperability. https://www.etsi.org/deliver/etsi_gr/PDL/001_099/006/01.01.01_60/gr_PDL006v010101p.pdf. Accessed 15 Dec 2022

Etzioni A (2019) Cyber trust. J Bus Ethics 156:1–13. https://doi.org/10.1007/s10551-017-3627-y

European Commission (2018) The user experience of the eIDAS-based eID. COM/DIGIT.D3/ 2017/01-035

European Commission (2022) Study supporting the review of the application of the Web Accessibility Directive (WAD) VIGIE 2020-0656 Final report (October 2022). https://ec.europa.eu/ newsroom/dae/redirection/document/92155. Accessed 16 Dec 2022

European Commission (2023) The European digital identity wallet architecture and reference framework. https://digital-strategy.ec.europa.eu/en/library/european-digital-identity-wallet-architecture-and-reference-framework. Accessed 8 Mar 2023

Floridi L (2020) The fight for digital sovereignty: what it is, and why it matters, especially for the EU. Philos Technol 33(3):369–378

Goldacker G (2017) Digitale Souveränität. Fraunhofer FOKUS. Digitale Souveränität (oeffentliche-it.de). Accessed 14 Dec 2022

Inglesant P, Sasse MA (2007) Usability is the best policy: public policy and the lived experience of transport systems in London. In: Proceedings of HCI 2007 The 21st British HCI Group Annual Conference University of Lancaster, UK (HCI)

ISA2 (2019) European Taxonomy for public services. Directorate-General for Informatics Directorate B — Interoperability Solutions for public administrations, businesses and citizens Unit B6 — ISA2 Programme. https://ec.europa.eu/isa2/news/new-level-cooperation-isa-building-inter operable-europe_en/. Accessed 12 Dec 2022

von Lucke J, Reinermann H (2002) Speyerer definition von electronic government. In: Heinrich Reinermann/Jörn von Lucke (Hrsg.), Electronic government in Deutschland, vol 226. Speyerer Forschungsberichte. Speyer 2002, S. pp 1–8

Kubach M, Roßnagel H (2021) A lightweight trust management infrastructure for self-sovereign identity. In: Roßnagel H, Schunck CH, Mödersheim S (eds) Open Identity Summit 2021. Gesellschaft für Informatik e.V., Bonn, pp 155–166

Kubicek H, Cimander R, Scholl HJ (2011) Organizational interoperability in e-government. Lessons from 77 European good-practice cases. Springer, Berlin

Martinez Jurado V, Vila X, Kubach M et al (2021) Applying assurance levels when issuing and verifying credentials using Trust Frameworks. In: Roßnagel H, Schunck CH, Mödersheim S (eds) Open Identity Summit 2021. Gesellschaft für Informatik e.V., Bonn, pp 167–178

Meijer A, Bekkers V (2015) A metatheory of e-government: creating some order in a fragmented research field. Gov Inf Quart 32(3):237–245

Meijer A, Bolívar MPR, Gil-Garcia JR (2018) From e-government to digital era governance and beyond: lessons from 15 years of research into information and communications technology in the public sector. J Publ Admin Res Theory:1–6

Pardo TA, Nam T, Burke GB (2012) E-government interoperability: interaction of policy, management, and technology dimensions. Soc Sci Comput Rev 30(1):7–23

Pöhn D, Grabatin M, Hommel W (2021) eID and self-sovereign identity usage: an overview. Electronics 10(22):2811

Shehu A, Pinto A, Correia ME (2019) On the interoperability of European National Identity Cards. In: Novais P, Jung JJ, Villarrubia González G et al (eds) Advances in intelligent systems and computing. Ambient Intelligence – Software and Applications – 9th International Symposium on Ambient Intelligence, vol 806. Springer International, Cham, pp 338–348

Spyrou A, Kaklanis N, Tzovaras D et al (2019) WADcher: a unified web accessibility assessment framework. SMART ACCESSIBILITY 2019, The Fourth International Conference on Universal Accessibility in the Internet of Things and Smart Environments, Athens, Greece. https:// zenodo.org/record/2604316. Accessed 16 Dec 2022

Strüker J, Urbach N, Guggenberger T et al (2021) Self-Sovereign Identity – Grundlagen, Anwendungen und Potenziale portabler digitaler Identitäten. Projektgruppe Wirtschaftsinformatik des Fraunhofer-Instituts für Angewandte Informationstechnik FIT, Bayreuth

Tenhunen S (2022) Revision of the eIDAS Regulation. Findings on its implementation and application. European Parliamentary Research Service (EPRS). https://www.europarl.europa.eu/RegData/etudes/BRIE/2022/699491/EPRS_BRI(2022)699491_EN.pdf.   Accessed 6 Jan 2023

Tobin A, Reed D (2016) The inevitable rise of self-sovereign identity. The Sovrin Foundation. https://sovrin.org/wp-content/uploads/2018/03/The-Inevitable-Rise-of-Self-Sovereign-Identity.pdf. Accessed 11 Jan 2023

Chapter 3
Data Privacy and Security in Online Public Services

This chapter reviews the state of the art of data privacy and security, including the latest discussions, good practices and threats in online public services. Departing from the case of the European Union, it focuses on the German e-government context.

The chapter clarifies the meaning of the terms data privacy and security. Both terms are often used interchangeably; however, they mean different things. Data privacy refers to how data are collected, used, archived, shared and deleted in accordance with the law. For example, in 2018, the European Union (EU) enacted the General Data Protection Regulation (GDPR) to govern the collection of personal information, including phone numbers, biometric data, IP addresses and so on. Security, on the other hand, relates to how information is protected. This means the implementation of technical safeguards used to ensure the confidentiality, integrity and availability of data.

The chapter also briefly covers the controversies on data privacy and protection between the EU and the USA.[1]

3.1 The Meaning of the Terms Data Privacy and Security

The increasing collection of citizens' data to facilitate the usage of OPS brings different risks for the stakeholders involved in data delivery, collection and processing (citizens, businesses, government administrations, IT service providers, etc.). Data privacy and security are thus indispensable aspects in the design development and evaluation of OPS. Data privacy concerns how data are collected, used, archived, shared and deleted in accordance with the law. Data privacy is thus defined

---

[1] See, i.e. https://insidecybersecurity.com/sites/insidecybersecurity.com/files/documents/may2016/cs2016_0076.pdf (accessed 12 Sep 2022).

E. Ruiz Ben, M. Scholl, *Usable Privacy and Security in Online Public Services*,
https://doi.org/10.1007/978-3-031-43383-2_3

within a particular national or multinational legal framework. This means that the legal basis of data privacy must be understood in relation to the cultural, social and political understanding of privacy of the specific national contexts where it is defined.

The concept of privacy also differs from one historical time to another. Therefore, for example, the relation between privacy and data is relatively new as well as the relation between information and security and the complexities of responsibilities that concern different actors in specific political arenas of data protection (i.e. responsibilities of individuals as citizens, of governments as public service providers, of IT companies as IT service platform providers in democratic countries in the EU). To what extent are data private, and who has the responsibility to protect them? These questions concern the political debate and the legal basis established in national or multinational contexts.

Data or information security—sometimes used synonymously—on the other hand, basically refers to the ways in which data or information is protected against misuse.

This is just an approximative idea of the differentiation between both areas of usable privacy and security. However, these concepts overlap and sometimes even contradict each other in many situations. Moreover, there are several complexities in the definitions of data, their level of sensitivity, the protection of metadata, the conceptualisation and limitation of privacy and the standardisation of security methods (see Anderson 2020, Chap. 1, for a detailed explanation) that affect both data privacy and information security. In the next sections, we aim to disentangle some of these complexities. We begin with the concept of data privacy to continue with the concept and standards of data and information security.

3.1.1   Data Privacy

The prohibition data privacy principle has long applied as data protection laws, especially in Germany, since 1970: Any processing of personal data requires a legal basis that permits or orders it or the fact that the data subject has given (written) consent; otherwise, the processing of personal data is unlawful. Data protection laws such as the European General Data Protection Regulation (GDPR) have been at the top since 2018. This is followed in Germany by the Federal Data Protection Act (BDSG), the state laws (LDSG) and other special legal regulations depending on the area of application. All data protection laws contain authorisations for the processing of personal data that are otherwise prohibited.

The concept of data privacy connects the principles of privacy in society with the allowed processes of data collection, usage, archiving, sharing and deletion under law. Both aspects of data privacy must be contextualised in the particular social context in which they are legitimised. For example, data privacy in the framework of the EU General Data Protection Regulation has a different legitimate background than in the USA with their more fragmented legal approach of regulation (de Bruin et al. 2022).

Privacy very basically concerns different aspects of social life, including physical and psychological dimensions. It concerns the relationship between individuals and the collective assuming the autonomy of individuals (Blume 2010). Privacy is one of the values on which some justice theories are grounded, bounded in specific social and national contexts and in concrete historical moments (Blume 2010). In some historical moments, privacy may have no importance, whereas in others, it is a prior value for defining justice. The concept of privacy assumes that individuals have a certain autonomy and a degree of control with respect to other members of the collective to which individuals belong. From a physical perspective, this basically means control over the space individuals inhabit, their home. This old idea has evolved to include other immaterial aspects of individual life in the realms of society. This is related to the ideas and information of/about an individual, in the sense that when the use of this information may harm the person's integrity and autonomy, information about individuals becomes part of individual privacy and justice.

With the increasing usage and exchange of personal data on the internet, this immaterial privacy dimension has become crucial in social lives as well as its regulation in terms of the extent to which information and data about individuals may be used. Nevertheless, data protection is not a self-evident principle but an ideological and social one. In many societies, privacy does not even constitute a basic right (Blume 2010). In societies ruled by liberal and democratic ideologies, privacy constitutes a major value and justice principle, whereas in other societies ruled, for example, by authoritarian regimes, privacy is not a priority value. Moreover, the technological stage in particular nations may enable a more sophisticated degree of privacy than in others.

Another important aspect related to privacy is individual consent (Solove 2008: 1880 ff.). Laws for protecting data privacy are basically based upon the provision of rights to individuals for autonomously deciding about the management of their data. These rights include notice, access and consent in relation to the collection, usage and disclosure of personal data. Solove (2008) contends that privacy self-management based on personal consent does not provide individuals with appropriate tools to protect their data. Cognitive and structural problems as well as social-related conflicts prevent appropriate data privacy protection. Cognitive problems relate to the abilities of individuals to make "informed, rational choices about the costs and benefits of consenting to the collection, use and disclosure of their personal data" (Solove 2008: 1881). Individuals do not have equal digital competences and skills (e.g. the concept of the "digital divide")[2] and in many cases cannot totally understand what they consent and with which consequences. Solove (2008) also refers to structural problems in terms of the numerous nonexplicit added entities operating in the processing of data on the internet that individuals cannot be aware

---

[2] https://www.utwente.nl/en/centrefordigitalinclusion/Blog/02-Digitale_Kloof/.   Accessed 13 Dec 2022

of. These entities may operate not just once but in different periods and in aggregated form, so it is not possible to have an overview of the spatial and time-bounded consequences of consenting in data privacy terms. The harms of using individuals' data are often not limited to individual persons but affect a whole society and the modelling of its complexities and solutions. Solove (2008) remarks that governments tend to rely on individual consent or paternalistic policies to solve these complexities.

Four main problems are connected with the prioritisation of individual consent in data privacy policies: first, people do not read privacy policies; second, even if people read these policies, they do not understand them; third, if people read and even understand them, they may lack the background knowledge necessary to make informed decisions; and fourth, if people read the policies, understand them and have background knowledge to make informed decisions, they might fail due to decision-making difficulties.

Even in this pessimistic panorama, Solove (2008) supports self-management in data privacy protection and encourages improving consumers' education as well as the delivery of clearer notices and choices. This is not because these are the most effective solutions to the consent and self-management dilemmas in data privacy protection but because they might prevent companies from indiscriminately collecting and using private data.

It is also important to consider that privacy and data protection are not totally equivalent. Data protection is an instrument to protect the broader concept of privacy that not only covers the processing of personal information. Data protection is, however, broader in scope than privacy since it concerns any kind of data processing independently of whether it interferes with the privacy of the individuals (De Hert et al. 2012).

Data privacy also includes the protection of autonomy and control over data subjects' personal information/data in interactions with public organisations and authorities (e-government C2G). IT service providers must also be considered at this point since the government administrations themselves do not develop the OPS systems and infrastructures alone. Governments very much depend on an "ecosystem" of IT companies and businesses cooperating with public administrations to deliver OPS. In other words, data privacy regulations are mechanisms that protect individuals' autonomy and control over their own data against private and public surveillance. In the next section, we concentrate on the implementation of the GDPR in the EU that governs the collection of personal information, including phone numbers, biometric data, IP addresses and so on, which is crucial for understanding the basic aspects of e-government in the delivery of OPS mentioned before: trust and transparency.

3.1.2   *Data Privacy and the GDPR in the Delivery of OPS*

In the past, the postal address was a major identifier for companies' customers. In the digital era, the most important identifiers are personal email addresses, phone numbers and smartphone IDs. Other ways of identifying customers' information are the calculation of digital fingerprints from behavioural data such as website visits, places visited, apps in use, videos viewed, purchase history or contacts added to digital communication devices. For using OPS, we have explained in Chap. 2 the importance of digital identities as identifiers. More concretely, we have referred to eID and its regulation with eIDAS in the e-government context of the EU.

The usage of data collected by communication system providers to identify their customers in the USA and in the UK is not supported in the same way within the EU. Data privacy is very differently conceptualised and legally protected in these national and supranational contexts. US surveillance law requests data from US companies collected from foreign customers on demand (Esteve 2017). The EU General Data Protection Regulation (GDPR)[3] focuses on data privacy protection (Anderson 2020). In contrast to the GDPR approach to protect privacy at a multinational and supranational level, in the USA, there is not a single legal framework for data privacy protection.[4]

In the EU, the GDPR that entered into force in 2018 serves as a common legal base for data privacy protection. In particular, Article 5 of the GDPR[5] covers basic principles of data processing. These are the following: lawfulness, fairness, transparency, purpose limitation, data minimisation, accuracy, storage limitation, confidentiality and accountability. These principles apply in the design and implementation of OPS and their eID access facilities referred to in the previous chapter. Table 3.1[6] shows an overview of the main aspects of the GDPR that affect the delivery of OPS. In general terms, personal data processing under the GDPR is based upon opting-in, including a data subject's deliberate action (e.g. choosing from equally prominent options), which means that processing personal data must be explicitly consented to by the data subject.

In general terms, personal data processing under the GDPR is based upon opting-in, including a data subject's deliberate action (e.g. choosing from equally prominent options), which means that processing personal data must be explicitly consented to by the data subject. As the European Data Protection Board (EDPB) remarks in

---

[3] https://eur-lex.europa.eu/legal-content/EN/TXT/PDF/?uri=CELEX:32016R0679&from=EN. Accessed 3 Jan 2023

[4] https://www.nytimes.com/wirecutter/blog/state-of-privacy-laws-in-us/ and https://iapp.org/media/pdf/resource_center/State_Comp_Privacy_Law_Chart.pdf. Accessed 8 Mar 2023

[5] https://eur-lex.europa.eu/legal-content/EN/TXT/?uri=CELEX%3A32016R0679&qid=16692 85919230. Accessed 24 Nov 2022

[6] https://commission.europa.eu/law/law-topic/data-protection/reform/rules-business-and-organisa tions/public-administrations-and-data-protection/what-are-main-aspects-general-data-protection-regulation-gdpr-public-administration-should-be-aware_en. Accessed 2 Jan 2023

Table 3.1 Key aspects of the GDPR for public administrations

Data processing basis	– Legal obligation – Need to perform tasks carried out in public interest – Need to perform tasks carried out in the exercise of official authority
Prior to processing data	Individuals must be informed about processing purpose, types of data collected, the recipients (all organisations or companies receiving individuals' personal data) and their data protection rights (access, correction, deletion, complaint, data portability,[a] withdrawal of consent)
Key principles of data processing (see GDPR Art 5)	– Fair, transparent and lawful processing – Purpose limitation – Data minimisation – Accuracy – Storage limitation – Integrity and confidentiality
Appointment of data protection officer (DPO) (see GDPR Art 37–39)	A single officer may be assigned to several public bodies or outsource this work to an external DPO
Implementation of data security measures (information security)	– Ensure that the appropriate organisational and technical measures to secure personal data are implemented. This includes external organisations ("processors", s. GDPR Art 28) where parts of the processing might have been outsourced – Guarantee of processors' data security obligation according to GDPR with a contract or another legal act
Obligation to notify breach to data protection authority (DPA) (see GDPR Art. 4)	Without undue delay at latest within 72 h after becoming aware of the breach. Public administration may need to inform individuals about the breach

[a]https://europa.eu/youreurope/citizens/consumers/internet-telecoms/data-protection-online-privacy/index_en.htm. Accessed 4 Jan 2023

reference to GDPR Recital 43, there is a clear imbalance of power between controllers and data subjects regarding the free given consent established in Art 4(11). Mostly, the data subjects have no other option than to accept the processing terms of the controllers. The EDPB recommends referring to other lawful bases (GDPR Art 6 (1c, 1e), complying with a legal obligation or performing a task carried out in the public interest) (EDPB 2020b). This is particularly the case in OPS. In Chap. 4, we will explain in more detail this challenge in the design of usable secure OPS.

Chapter III of the GDPR covers individuals' rights on data privacy: access, rectification, erasure, restriction, objection and right not to be object to automated decision-making. The right to object to the processing of personal data by public administrations is based upon public interest. This means that individuals must provide reasons regarding their situation for objecting to the processing of their personal data. However, public administrations, including controllers, may deny individuals' requests if they base personal data processing on legitimate grounds or "for the establishment, exercise or defence of legal claims" (s. GDPR Art 21).

In any case, individuals' requests to public administrations about personal data processing must be answered without undue delay and within 1 month of receiving the request.[7] The tools that apply if the public administration fails to comply with the GDPR include warning, reprimand or temporary or definitive ban on the processing or administrative fines.[8]

Public administrations, including controllers[9] and processors, must inform individuals beforehand about personal data processing in OPS usage. At this point, it is important to consider the distinction between the roles of these actors in the personal data processing related to the usage of OPS in the EU. To put it simply, controllers are the decision-makers, and processors act on the instructions and behalf of the controllers in data processing.[10] However, as Santos et al. (2021) remark, the roles of both actors sometimes overlap. According to GDPR Recital 42, at least the identity of the controller must be provided to the data subjects.

The European Data Protection Board (EDPB) remarks that as part of consent requirements, processors do not need to be named. However, to comply with GDPR Arts 13 and 14, controllers need to include a full list of data recipients, including processors (EDPB 2020b).

Information about cookies must also be provided, and individuals' consent to install them in their computers must be held by personal data recipients as well. However, not all cookies need to be consented to by individuals. This is the case for those cookies used to carry out the transmission of communication.[11]

Important aspects of the GDPR directly related to usable privacy and security are the individuals' right to be informed prior to the processing of their personal data and the way in which public administration informs data subjects about data processing. The GDPR makes clear that individuals must be informed using clear and plain language and consent must be freely given (s. GDPR Art 7). This includes that the individuals must have the choice of refusing or withdrawing their consent without any detriment (s. GDPR Recital 42). We will return to these aspects in the next chapter when we explain the usable privacy and security challenges in OPS delivery.

---

[7] https://commission.europa.eu/law/law-topic/data-protection/reform/rules-business-and-organisations/public-administrations-and-data-protection/how-should-requests-individuals-be-dealt_en. Accessed 3 Jan 2023

[8] https://commission.europa.eu/law/law-topic/data-protection/reform/rules-business-and-organisations/public-administrations-and-data-protection/how-should-requests-individuals-be-dealt_en. Accessed 3 Jan 2023

[9] "'Controller' means the natural or legal person, public authority, agency or other body which, alone or jointly with others, determines the purposes and means of the processing of personal data" (GDPR Recital 7).

[10] https://ico.org.uk/for-organisations/guide-to-data-protection/guide-to-the-general-data-protection-regulation-gdpr/key-definitions/controllers-and-processors/. Accessed 4 Jan 2023

[11] https://europa.eu/youreurope/citizens/consumers/internet-telecoms/data-protection-online-privacy/index_en.htm. Accessed 4 Jan 2023

3.2   Data Security

Data security (synonymously used as information security or data protection, although these terms are to be differentiated) relates to how information is protected.[12] This includes the implementation of technical safeguards used to ensure the confidentiality, integrity and availability of data. The definition of data security varies between different international data protection organisations. For example, the US National Institute of Standards and Technology (NIST) defines information security as "The protection of information and information systems from unauthorized access, use, disclosure, disruption, modification, or destruction in order to provide confidentiality, integrity, and availability".[13]

The ISO/IEC 27000:2018 uses a narrower definition: "preservation of confidentiality, integrity and availability of information". The EU Cybersecurity Act (CSA) refers to "cybersecurity" in more general terms as "activities necessary to protect network and information systems, the users of such systems, and other persons affected by cyberthreats" (Andrukiewicz et al. 2021).

Particularly, security engineering focuses on those data protection aspects but also on the identification of the specific data that must be protected and how, since this can very much differ from one application context to another (Anderson 2008). According to Anderson (2008), good security engineering requires four main inter-related things: first, a policy establishing the security achievements; second, the mechanisms to implement the policy; third, the assurance, meaning the amount of reliance to place in each mechanism; and fourth, the incentive for the engineers to properly accomplish their job.

In the case of OPSs, from a data subject perspective, private data exchanged in e-government interactions and authentication credentials, including those data sets to be introduced into the planned EUDI Wallet,[14] are the most important assets to protect. In the EU context, GDPR Article 5 refers to the data security targets: availability, integrity and confidentiality. The *availability* includes the specific findability of data; the ability of the technical systems used to present data in an appropriate manner, including for people; and the interpretability of the content of the data. For *integrity*, there is a requirement that there is sufficient coverage between the legal and normative requirements and actual practice. The guarantee objective of *confidentiality* describes the requirement that no unauthorised person can gain

---

[12] Cybersecurity has a broader scope than data protection. For an overview of the current legislation on cybersecurity as well as on the various agencies involved in the implementation of cybersecurity across the EU, see https://digital-strategy.ec.europa.eu/en/policies/cybersecurity-policies (accessed 1 Mar 2023).

[13] https://csrc.nist.gov/glossary/term/infosec. Accessed 1 Mar 2023

[14] In addition to the mandatory eIDAS attributes current family name, current first names, date of birth and unique identifier, the EUDI Wallet may additionally contain information about nationality/citizenship and optional attributes used at national level, e.g. tax number, social security number, etc. See page 22 in https://digital-strategy.ec.europa.eu/en/library/european-digital-identity-wallet-architecture-and-reference-framework (accessed 2 Mar 2023).

knowledge of personal data. The guarantee goal of *integrity* describes the requirement that personal data may not be merged, i.e. chained.

Regarding how to protect personal data in OPSs, in the EU context, Article 32 of the GDPR addresses the security of the processing of personal data and includes aspects such as pseudonymisation and encryption, the resilience of the systems, data recovery, the instruction of subordinate employees and a regular review, assessment and evaluation of the effectiveness of technical and organisational measures (TOM). Associated with this is a risk-based approach for an adequate level of protection. As a minimum, ten different TOMs must be established by the processor that ensure that the aspects defined in GDPR Article 32 are guaranteed. The background and the focus of data protection are given in GDPR Recital 75.

The Senior Officials Group Information Systems Security (SOG-IS) in the EU context has elaborated a document with specific cryptographic mechanisms agreed upon among several EU member states to be applied among others for data protection of OPS in the EU, including the planned EUDI Wallet.[15]

Another data security mechanism in the specific framework of OPS is the implementation of a comprehensive privacy risk management plan by public administrations (including controllers and processors). The requirements for this plan covered in the GDPR are as follows:

- Data protection by design and by default (s. GDPR Art 25)
- Documentation of the personal data held and personal data processing activities (s. GDPR Art 30)
- Data protection impact assessment (DPIA) (s. GDPR Art 35)
- Appointment of a data protection officer (DPO) (s. GDPR Art 37–39)

Data protection by design relates to the obligation for controllers to implement technical and organisational measures for personal data privacy protection from the very beginning of the data processing procedures design. Data protection by default means that only those personal data necessary for each specific processing purpose (the amount of personal data collected, the extent of their processing, the period of storage and their accessibility) will be processed (s. GDPR Art 25). Both concepts are complementary and reinforce each other. The EDPB has published a set of guidelines related to both aspects of the GDPR (EDPB 2020a). In the next chapter, we comment on these guidelines that are important to face the challenges of usable privacy and security to support digital sovereignty in the context of e-government and the delivery of OPS.

---

[15] https://www.sogis.eu/documents/cc/crypto/SOGIS-Agreed-Cryptographic-Mechanisms-1.2.pdf. Accessed 2 Mar 2023

3.3   Summary

- Data privacy concerns how data are collected, used, archived, shared and deleted in accordance with the law.
- Data or information security—sometimes used synonymously—basically refers to the ways in which data or information is protected against misuse.
- With the increasing usage and exchange of personal data on the internet, the immaterial dimension of privacy has become crucial in social lives as well as its regulation in terms of the extent to which information and data about individuals may be used.
- Data privacy regulations are mechanisms that protect individuals' autonomy and control over their own data against private and public surveillance.
- In the EU, the GDPR that entered into force in 2018 serves as a common legal base for data privacy protection. In particular, Article 5 of the GDPR[16] covers the basic principles of data processing. These are the following: lawfulness, fairness, transparency, purpose limitation, data minimisation, accuracy, storage limitation, confidentiality and accountability.
- Important aspects of the GDPR directly related to usable privacy and security are individuals' right to be informed prior to the processing of their personal data and the way in which public administration informs data subjects about data processing.
- Data or information security includes the implementation of technical safeguards used to ensure the confidentiality, integrity and availability of data.
- In the case of OPSs, from a data subject perspective, private data exchanged in e-government interactions and authentication credentials, including those data sets to be introduced into the planned EUDI Wallet,[17] are the most important assets to protect.
- Another data security mechanism in the specific framework of OPS is the implementation of a comprehensive privacy risk management plan by public administrations (including controllers and processors).

---

[16] https://eur-lex.europa.eu/legal-content/EN/TXT/?uri=CELEX%3A32016R0679&qid=16692 85919230. Accessed 24 Nov 2022

[17] In addition to the mandatory eIDAS attributes current family name, current first names, date of birth and unique identifier, the EUDI Wallet may additionally contain information about nationality/ citizenship and optional attributes used at national level, e.g. tax number, social security number, etc. See page 22 in https://digital-strategy.ec.europa.eu/en/library/european-digital-identity-wallet-architecture-and-reference-framework (accessed 2 Mar 2023).

3.4 Examples and Exercises

3.4.1 Examples

An example of the implementation of a tool for delivering GDPR-conforming OPSs in a smart city is available at Daoudagh et al. (2021).

Another example of a usable privacy and security tool for implementing GDPR-conforming downloads is available at Veys et al. (2021).

3.4.2 Exercises: Can You Explain? (Check Yourself)

1. What are the basic principles of data processing according to Article 5 of the GDPR?
2. These principles apply to the design and implementation of OPS and its eID access facilities. Identify the key aspects of the GDPR that impact the delivery of OPS.

Glossary

Availability "Ensuring timely and reliable access to and use of information" [https://csrc.nist.gov/glossary/term/availability (accessed 8 Mar 2023)].

Confidentiality "Preserving authorized restrictions on information access and disclosure, including means for protecting personal privacy and proprietary information" [https://csrc.nist.gov/glossary/term/confidentiality (accessed 8 Mar 2023)].

Integrity "Guarding against improper information modification or destruction, and includes ensuring information non-repudiation and authenticity" [https://csrc.nist.gov/glossary/term/integrity (accessed 8 Mar 2023)].

Personal Information or Data Any information relating to an identified or identifiable natural (living) person. Examples include names, dates of birth, photographs, video footage, email addresses and telephone numbers. Other details, such as IP addresses and communications content—related to or provided by end-users of communications services—are also considered personal data. See https://edps.europa.eu/press-publications/press-news/press-releases/2020/euro pean-commissions-gdpr-review-stronger_en (accessed 20 Oct 2022).

Further Reading

Andrukiewicz E, Atallah E, Bartels C et al (2021) Methodology for sectoral cybersecurity assessments. EU cybersecurity certification framework. ENISA. https://doi.org/10.2824/490490

EDPB (2022) Guidelines 01/2022 on data subject rights – Right of access. https://edpb.europa.eu/system/files/2022-01/edpb_guidelines_012022_right-of-access_0.pdf. Accessed 8 Mar 2023

References

Anderson RA (2008) Security engineering: a guide to building dependable distributed systems. Wiley, London

Anderson R (2020) Security engineering: a guide to building dependable distributed systems, 3rd edn. John Wiley & Sons, Hoboken, NJ

Andrukiewicz E, Atallah E, Bartels C et al (2021) Methodology for sectoral cybersecurity assessments. EU cybersecurity certification framework. ENISA. https://doi.org/10.2824/490490

Blume P (2010) Data protection and privacy–basic concepts in a changing world. Scandinavian Stud Law. ICT Legal Issues 56:151–164

Daoudagh S, Marchetti E, Savarino V et al (2021) Data protection by design in the context of smart cities: a consent and access control proposal. Sensors 21(21):7154. https://doi.org/10.3390/s21217154

de Bruin (2022) A comparative analysis of the EU and U.S. Data privacy regimes and the potential for convergence and the potential for convergence. Hastings Sci Technol Law J 13(2):126–157. Available at: https://repository.uchastings.edu/hastings_science_technology_law_journal/vol13/iss2/4. Accessed Oct 3, 2023

De Hert P, Kloza D, Wright D (2012) Recommendations for a privacy impact assessment framework for the European Union. https://biblio.ugent.be/publication/8738595. Accessed 9 Feb 2023

EDPB (2020a) Guidelines 4/2019 on Article 25 Data Protection by Design and by Default Version 2.0. Adopted on 20 October 2020. https://edpb.europa.eu/sites/default/files/files/file1/edpb_guidelines_201904_dataprotection_by_design_and_by_default_v2.0_en.pdf. Accessed 4 Jan 2023

EDPB (2020b) Guidelines 05/2020 on consent under Regulation 2016/679 Version 1.1. Adopted on 4 May 2020. https://edpb.europa.eu/sites/default/files/files/file1/edpb_guidelines_202005_consent_en.pdf. Accessed 4 Jan 2023

EDPB (2022) Guidelines 01/2022 on data subject rights – Right of access. https://edpb.europa.eu/system/files/2022-01/edpb_guidelines_012022_right-of-access_0.pdf. Accessed 8 Mar 2023

Esteve A (2017) The business of personal data: Google, Facebook, and privacy issues in the EU and the USA. Int Data Privacy Law 7(1):36–47. https://doi.org/10.1093/idpl/ipw026

Nair NV, Shaikh AU (2023) Privacy and data protection laws: an overview. IUP Law Rev 12(2): 51–57

Santos C, Nouwens M, Toth M, Bielova N, Roca V (2021) Consent management platforms under the GDPR: processors and/or controllers? APF 2021 – 9th Annual Privacy Forum, Jun 2021, Oslo, Norway, pp 47–69

Solove DJ (2008) Understanding privacy. In: GWU Legal Studies Research Paper No. 420, GWU Law School Public Law Research Paper No. 420. Harvard University Press. Available at SSRN: https://ssrn.com/abstract=1127888. Accessed Oct 3, 2023

Veys S, Serrano D, Stamos M et al (2021) Pursuing usable and useful data downloads under GDPR/CCPA access rights via co-design. https://www.usenix.org/system/files/soups2021-veys.pdf. Accessed 11 June 2023

Chapter 4
Challenges of Usable Privacy and Security in the Context of E-Government and Online Public Services

In the context of e-government and, more concretely, in the design, development and delivery of public services online, practitioners confront specific challenges to integrate usable privacy and security measures. First, the users of online public services are both citizens and public servants. Second, users of online public services are not a specific target group but a highly diversified population affected by several digital gaps. This chapter explains the main challenges derived from the need for inclusion in the usage of online public services of all citizens despite any digital gap (education, disabilities, language, etc.). A central concept for understanding the specific challenges of developing usable secure online public services in the context of e-government is digital sovereignty. The chapter begins with an explanation of this concept to further specify concrete related challenges for IT practitioners.

Solutions to these challenges, such as user participation, are conceptually explained in this chapter to prepare the more technical in-depth coverage of methodological approaches in the following chapter.

4.1 Digital Sovereignty in E-Government Contexts

The concept of digital sovereignty has been increasingly used with different connotations in recent years (Couture and Toupin 2019). One important reason for this increasing usage of the term is the competition between nations in the global digitalisation of social and economic life. The concept of digital sovereignty is used in different ways without a definition consensus (Müller et al. 2022). Basically, in Europe, the references to the concept can be categorised into three levels: the state, the economy and the individual (Pohle 2020).

In the contexts of e-governments and from a usable privacy and security perspective, it is important to consider the centrality of OPS users as sovereign digital citizens over their personal data. Couture and Toupin (2019) refer to five main forms of sovereignty in relation to digitalisation (cyberspace sovereignty, state digital sovereignty, indigenous digital sovereignty, social movement digital sovereignty and personal digital sovereignty). The most dominant concept of digital sovereignty refers to the capacity of nation-states to assert control over infrastructures residing within their territory and data produced by their citizens (Couture 2020). Floridi (2020: 370–371) expands this notion of digital sovereignty, emphasising the importance of the fight for the control of data, software, "...standards and protocols (e.g., 5G, domain names), processes (e.g., cloud computing), hardware (e.g., mobile phones), services (e.g., social media, e-commerce), and infrastructures (e.g., cables, satellites, smart cities), in short, for the control of the digital". Control in relation to digital sovereignty means the ability to influence something and its dynamic, including the ability to check and correct for any deviation from such influence (Floridi 2020: 371). Thus, control in these terms can be pooled but also transferred. This also means that control can be a form of individual sovereignty over one's own body, choices and data. From a citizens' perspective—users of OPS and data subjects—digital sovereignty refers to their confidence to control, use and understand digital facilities (BMWi 2021: 9).

Citizens' digital sovereignty in the context of OPS requires a mutual awareness and dialog between the state, the designers of the online public services and the citizens about forms of adoption and acceptance of digital services as well as about needs and responsibilities of the involved actors in the implementation and in data privacy and security. These are central usability topics. In the concrete context of e-government and OPS in the EU, the individual level of digital sovereignty (citizens and companies, as well as public administrations using OPS—soon mandatory through a single digital gateway) connects with the level of the state setting regulations and making decisions about technical solutions with economic partners (economic level) for delivering OPS in the EU.

In the EU understanding of digital sovereignty, although the EU Commission calls for stronger digital literacy and a conscious approach to digital technologies, these goals are secondarily conceived as a result of EU achievements as a global leader in the digital economy (Pohle 2020).

To develop usable OPS from a data privacy and security perspective, we conceive digital sovereignty departing from citizens' needs to use OPS (Table 4.1). To achieve digital sovereignty in the usage of OPS, it is essential to cover these needs. More concretely, in relation to data privacy and security, citizens need to be aware of the existence of legal and technical aspects. As digital sovereign citizens in control of their personal data, they need to understand these legal and technical aspects of data privacy and security and be able to act consequently. The five defined competence areas of the DigComp 2.1 report (Carretero et al. 2017) include some digital skills that support the understanding of the legal and technical aspects of data privacy and security, for example, in the competence area of communication and collaboration, the digital skill of managing digital identity, the fourth competence area of safety or the digital skills of protecting devices and protecting personal data and privacy.

From a usable privacy and security point of view, we need to consider the realities of the digital divide showing large disparities in the coverage of these needs to

Table 4.1 Features of digital sovereignty in OPS

Technological access	• Infrastructures such as broadband connection to access the internet • Digital devices – necessary for the planned usage of the EUDI Wallet; • Access to digital identities and attributes
Digital skills[a]	Competence areas: • Information data literacy • Communication and collaboration, • Digital content creation • Safety • Problem solving
OPS knowledge	• Stand of digitalisation of public services
Knowledge about data privacy and security	• Legal responsibilities and citizens' rights related to data privacy and security (GDPR). • Data privacy and security related to digital identities
Digital identities and attributes knowledge	• What are digital identities? What role do they play to use OPS? • How to manage and control digital identities and attributes?

[a]See https://publications.jrc.ec.europa.eu/repository/bitstream/JRC106281/web-digcomp2.1pdf_ (online).pdf (accessed 17 Jan 2023) and https://www.cedefop.europa.eu/en/data-insights/digital-skills-challenges-and-opportunities#_what_are_digital_skills (accessed 17 Jan 2023)

achieve digital sovereignty among EU citizens. In 2019, only three out of ten EU citizens had above basic digital skills.[1]

Usable privacy and security alone cannot compensate for these disparities, but it can contribute to helping data subjects to be aware of data privacy and security risks. Moreover, ignoring the usability (i.e. user control and freedom, error prevention, flexibility and efficiency, aesthetic and minimalism in design) of OPS affects all users, including digitally skilled citizens. The complexities of delivering OPS in a multinational environment of the EU will certainly increase in the next years (i.e. with the EUDI Wallet implementation), and with them, the requirements for citizens' digital skills will also grow. For designers of OPS, responsibilities have also grown in this respect. They must apply the mentioned concepts of data privacy by design and by default already acknowledged in the GDPR Art 25 (see Chap. 3) and use clear and plain language to provide information about data privacy and security.

We should also keep in mind that these challenges in the design and development of OPS in the context of e-government also affect public servants as well as public organisations and enterprises since they also use OPS. In the next section, we concentrate on the challenges that designers confront while developing OPS from a usable privacy and security perspective.

---

[1] https://www.cedefop.europa.eu/en/data-insights/digital-skills-challenges-and-opportunities#_digi tal_divide_in_the_eu. Accessed 17 Jan 2023

4.2   Challenges of Usable Privacy and Security in the Delivery of OPS

A departing point to define the challenges of usable privacy and security in the delivery of OPS are the institutionalised principles of information privacy and security in several governments and international organisations (the Organisation for Economic Co-operation and Development (OECD), the International Organization for Standardization (ISO), the EU, the Canadian Institute of Chartered Accountants and the American Institute of Certified Public Accountants. Comparing the privacy and security principles considered by these organisations, Multimukwe et al. (2019) have elaborated a classification into seven categories:

- Notice and awareness
- Access and user control
- Storage limitation
- Safeguard
- Accuracy and security
- Enforcement
- Accountability

Two of these categories, notice and awareness and access and user control, are particularly connected to usable privacy and security (how to give access to online services and inform about data privacy and security in an effective, efficient and satisfactory way for the data subjects). In the next section, we concentrate on the challenges related to usability and data privacy, more concern with the design of usable data privacy notice and awareness, access and user control in the context of e-government and OPS.

4.2.1   Challenges Related to Data Privacy in OPS

In the last chapters, we have discussed the topics of usability, data privacy and information security in the framework of e-government, focusing on the delivery of OPS in the case of the EU. From this discussion, we can extract the following challenges in the usable and secure delivery of OPS:

- OPS platform design for all citizens, public servants and enterprises: The design of the platforms and the artefacts to manage the digital identities and attributes needed to access OPS should follow the principles of the Web Accessibility Directive (WAD) included in the WCAG 2.1 (s. Chap. 2): perceivability, operability, understandability and robustness.
- Digital identity information for all citizens, public servants and enterprises: Prior to data processing, the platform and the artefacts to manage the digital identities and attributes should provide comprehensible, clear, effective and easy-to-learn

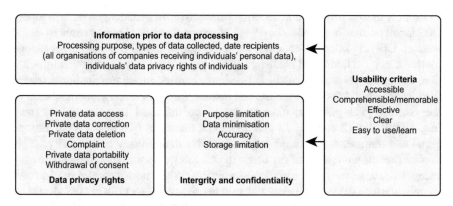

Fig. 4.1 Usable privacy in the delivery of OPS

information about the processing purpose, types of data collected, the recipients (all organisations or companies receiving individuals' personal data) and their data protection rights (access, correction, deletion, complaint, data portability,[2] withdrawal of consent).

- Digital identity platforms for all citizens, public servants and enterprises: The design of the platforms and the artefacts to manage digital identities and attributes needed to access the OPS must meet the needs of all citizens. This includes citizens with different digital skills and socioeconomic and cultural backgrounds as well as other actors involved in the delivery of OPS, such as public servants occupied in the delivery process of public services on the internet.

Figure 4.1 summarises the interrelated challenges to be considered in the design and development of usable secure OPS. Usability criteria applied to OPS enable and support users to make conscious informed data privacy and security decisions knowing and understanding their data privacy rights and the principles of lawful data processing.

These challenges can be only partially confronted with usable privacy and security methods. It is, for instance, assumed that all citizens have equal access to digital artefacts, including smartphones, to manage their digital identities and attributes (s. Chap. 3) needed to access OPS. However, as the research results of Rodríguez-Hevía et al. (2022) reveal, EU regional differences in digital skills affect the use of e-government facilities such as OPS. In less developed areas of the EU, information-search skills, problem-solving and use of software to manipulate content are the variables with the highest effect on the probability of using e-government facilities. In more developed areas of the EU, the probability of using e-government facilities is more affected by communication skills.

---

[2] https://europa.eu/youreurope/citizens/consumers/internet-telecoms/data-protection-online-privacy/index_en.htm. Accessed 4 Jan 2023

From a usable privacy and security perspective, the challenges of developing OPS for all citizens begin with the design of access channels to public services on the internet. Offering information about the status quo of the OPS is the first challenge for designers. An additional challenge at this point is the way to offer this information. For example, as we explain in previous chapters, in the multinational framework of the OPS delivery in the EU and looking forwards to the implementation of the single digital gateway, citizens should be informed in a transparent way (e.g. GDPR Art 12 and Art 13 and 14) about the status quo of the Your Europe portal and the access and usage implications for data privacy and security.[3] This implies that the navigation of the single digital gateway portal should facilitate easy access to data privacy and security information. While information provision and compliance with the laws are essential, usable privacy and security in OPS should go beyond focusing on persons' needs and their interactions with the OPS systems' privacy and security interfaces (Schaub and Cranor 2020). The content organisation, user experience, graphs, list, navigation and screen (Venkatesh et al. 2014) are, for example, important usability aspects to facilitate access to data privacy information in OPS portals.

The next challenge is the management of the digital identities and attributes to access the OPS on the internet. As we explained in Chap. 3, at the moment, citizens and business have access to OPS in the EU (2023) with three different methods depending on the sensitivity of the data required for the specific OPS they want to use. The scarcely adopted eID provides access to all available OPS. Another access method requires the creation and management of a password. Information about the data privacy risks and responsibilities of the stakeholders should be provided in a transparent way here too. Lawfulness of data processing (s. GDPR Art 5) applies here regarding the information that the data subject should provide in relation to these alternative identification methods for eID usage. The challenge for portal developers and designers from a usable privacy perspective is to ensure that the data subjects understand and are aware of the functionalities related to each of the identification and authentication methods and of their different data privacy implications. Moreover, due to the need to use transparent and clear language, the terminology related to the access procedures to OPS and the associated management of the digital identities and attributes should be explained (e.g. the meaning of identification, authentication, data integrity, data confidentiality, anonymisation and pseudonymisation). These challenges also apply to the design of the planned EUDI Wallet. According to the W3C v1.1 model,[4] which sets the design guidelines for verifiable credentials (VCs) of the EUDI Wallet, the privacy spectrum in relation to VCs ranges from pseudonymous to strongly identified. Establishing a privacy grade is use case dependent. However, the W3C v1.1 model prevents various general data privacy and security risks (i.e. personally identifiable information,

---

[3] https://www.theparliamentmagazine.eu/news/article/single-digital-gateway. Accessed 13 Jan 2023

[4] https://www.w3.org/TR/vc-data-model. Accessed 3 Aug 2023

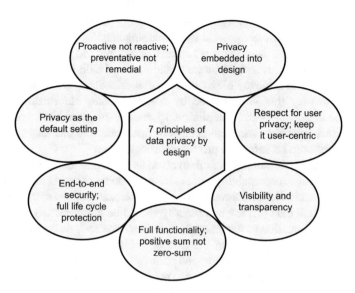

Fig. 4.2 The seven principles of data privacy by design (based on Cavoukian 2010a, b)

identity-based correlation, long-lived identity-based correlation, device fingerprinting, bearer credentials, validity checks, storage providers and data mining, aggregation of credentials, frequency of claim issuance and accessibility considerations). These aspects should be considered as an orientation to build adequate usable secure EUDI Wallets.

The early inclusion of citizens and public servants in the development of this new digital identity management method is necessary to avoid repeating the failures of the eID under the previous eIDAS (s. Chap. 2). An early exploration of users' mental models of this technology would also facilitate the development of usable privacy and security instruments and privacy by design and default (s. an example of SSI acceptance) (Korir et al. 2022).

In any case, controllers are required to offer data protection by design and by default, as we remarked in the last chapter. We explain these challenging aspects of usable privacy in relation to OPS in the next paragraphs: *data privacy by design and by default to support digital sovereignty (EDPB guidelines)*.

Data protection by design or privacy by design (PbD) refers to the steps included in the design of a software product, services or processes concentrated on the maintenance or preservation of the highest privacy standards. PbD assures the application of the highest privacy standards by using specific safeguards instruments and by considering data privacy and security through the whole development process (Cavoukian 2010a, b, 2012; Gürses and del Alamo 2016; Gürses et al. 2011). Cavoukian (2010a, b) summarised seven principles of data privacy by design that include privacy by default as well (see Fig. 4.2).

According to the principle "proactive and reactive; preventative not remedial", privacy risks should be anticipated and prevented before they happen. The principle of "privacy embedded into design" ensures that data privacy is integrated into the whole software development process by developing and implementing a systematic program. "Respect for user privacy" means designing and developing software products and services around the interests and needs of individual users. This is an essential principle to achieve PbD by offering user-friendly options and information about data privacy that is supported by several friendly information practices: consent, accuracy, access and compliance. Moreover, this principle emphasises the idea that human-machine interfaces need to be user-centric so that they enable users to consciously exercise informed privacy decisions.

"Visibility and transparency" of all involved technologies and business practices is needed to achieve accountability and assure every stakeholder. At the same time, it is necessary to avoid dichotomisations between, for example, the concepts of privacy and security. Both data privacy and security should be harmoniously conceived in PbD. This is the intention of the principle "full functionality". Accordingly, security measures should be applied from the start of the software products' or services' lifecycle to its end (principle "end-to-end security").

"Privacy as the default setting" refers to the automatic protection of personal data conceived from the beginning of the software and IT systems or services design. This principle implies that "no action is required on the part of the individual to protect their privacy – it is built into the system, by default" (Cavoukian 2010a, b: 4). Fair information practices related to this principle are purpose specification (of private data collection, use, retention and disclosure), private data collection limitation, data minimisation and use, retention and disclosure limitation. As we commented on in the previous chapter, the GDPR includes data privacy by design and by default. In our "Examples" section, we will show the cases of PbD adoption by the government of Canada.

All these data privacy challenges also apply to the design and development of the already mentioned SSIs in the EU. In particular, this new technology for managing digital identities brings additional challenges and uncertainties since the development is still rather fragmented. In addition to the challenge of creating an adequate eID ecosystem for EUDI Wallet implementation, the use of digital identities should be simple and self-determined but also as secure and privacy-friendly as possible and desirable, avoiding the creation of new lock-in effects. To achieve this, it is recommended to develop the ecosystem from the beginning in a transparent way for all citizens and stakeholders. Open-source software should be used, and the different solutions to develop SSIs for OPS should be discussed with the public. Usability is central for building trust in these SSI solutions (Wissenschaftliche Arbeitsgruppe Nationaler Cyber-Sicherheitsrat 2022). It is an open question whether these challenges will be sufficiently confronted and successfully solved. In any case, usability, security and privacy are likely to bring conflicts and dilemmas to the design (Halunen 2020). The divergences between the practices of software engineering and the proposals of privacy by design make it difficult to integrate privacy by design in the development of software products (Kostova et al. 2020). To solve the dilemmas of privacy by design in the practice of software engineering, Kostova et al. (2020) suggest building convergences between the siloed subdisciplines of computing.

An important aspect to build convergences in the practices and perspectives of the different groups involved in conceiving privacy by design in OPS is the definition of the end-users and the clear understanding of privacy and security responsibilities. For example, the users of OPS are all citizens, including public servants as well as public organisations and private companies. Risks and responsibilities on privacy and security are shared between all these actors, who to different extents are also involved in the development of the OPS themselves. The limits of these shared responsibilities are often difficult to grasp and frequently ignored. For example, software developers often believe that privacy and security are not relevant to certain products (Nurgalieva et al. 2021). Specific methods such as threat modelling exercises or vulnerability discovery activities are helpful to confront the challenge of acknowledging privacy and security responsibilities in the practice of software engineering, which also affect OPS designers and developers.

In the next section, we will explain some concrete methods and strategies for implementing PbD. The next section concentrates on the specific challenges related to data security in OPS.

4.2.2   Challenges Related to Data Security in OPS

In general, several specific challenges have been identified to achieve usable data security. The most salient are simplicity, information and support (feedback), task completion time, error rates and error management (Lennartsson et al. 2021). Simplicity refers in the usable data security literature reviewed by Lennartsson et al. (2021) to reducing the amount of required knowledge, the things users have to recall and the number of available choices and necessary decisions as well as the frequency of task-switching demands. As we will comment in the next chapter, task ordering and default configurations can be helpful to solve these challenges. Moreover, integrating security solutions into existing well-known systems and centralising authentication can be helpful as well to achieve the challenge of simplicity in data security. Regarding information and support, it is important that information about data security is understandable as well as findable and complete enough to address any potential problems related to functionalities. Another aspect related to the challenge of information provision about data security is the inclusion of explanations about the risks and benefits of security solutions. These explanations reduce usability issues and increase trust. Moreover, awareness of threats and their consequences can help to increase users' acceptance of security requirements as well as to a better system understanding and utilisation. Research on usable data security also reveals the importance of providing context-related information directly related to executed tasks that allows us to exhibit specifically required actions without interrupting the tasks, which reduces perceived complexity. A related aspect that also contributes to enhancing trust and reducing error rates is the feedback that should be provided to the users about underlying mechanisms, the progress of security actions, the system's status and the task completion (Lennartsson et al. 2021).

These general challenges of usable data security also apply to the specific context of OPSs and particularly to the safeguarding of data during authentication procedures[5] and usage of OPSs. From a multinational perspective, in the current once-only technical system (OOTS),[6] which is the technical framework for data sharing in the EU, eID and eDelivery are the central components for private data exchange related to OPS. The use of the eID (see Chap. 2) is one of the current options for authentication in OOTS, which is the first step in the user journey.[7] The challenges related to usable data security at this point include the simplicity in the provision of information and support for data security in the options to access OPSs in OOTS.[8]

A common challenge—particularly in light of the coming implementation of the single digital gateway and further for EUDI Wallet establishment in the EU—is the concretisation of data security measures for the multinational case as well as for single countries in the design of OPS.[9] Specifically, regarding data security, the W3C data model v1.1[10] refers to several aspects that designers and developers should account for, for example, in relation to the following aspects: content integrity protection, unsigned claims, token binding, bundling dependent claims, highly dynamic information, device theft and impersonation.

Technical and organisational measures for data protection by design and by default are not specified and must be adequate to the application context and to the risks related to the processing of the specific data used in the OPS. They should be appropriate and effective according to the data protection principles. The EDPB (2020) refers, for example, to several measures for implementing data protection by design:

---

[5] See https://ec.europa.eu/digital-building-blocks/wikis/display/TDD/Chapter+2%3A+User+Identi fication%2C+Authentication+and+Record+Matching+-+Q4+2022 for the explanations about users' identification and authentication in the framework of OOTS (accessed 3 Mar 2023).

[6] https://ec.europa.eu/digital-building-blocks/wikis/display/OOTS/OOTSHUB+Home.   Accessed 2 Mar 2023.

[7] https://ec.europa.eu/digital-building-blocks/wikis/display/OOTS/User+Journey+-+Step +1+Authentication. Accessed 2 Mar 2023.

[8] Both the EU Commission and the member states are responsible to ensure data security for the OOTS according to the Commission Implementing Regulation (EU) 2022/1463 of 5 August 2022 [https://eur-lex.europa.eu/legal-content/EN/TXT/?uri=uriserv%3AOJ.L_.2022.231.01.0001.01. ENG (accessed 2 Mar 2023)].

[9] The EU Cybersecurity Act, the EU NIS Directive and the new NIS2 as well as the EU single digital gateway regulation apply for the data security in OPS. Regarding the new NIS2, see https://www. consilium.europa.eu/en/press/press-releases/2022/11/28/eu-decides-to-strengthen-cybersecurity-and-resilience-across-the-union-council-adopts-new-legislation/ (accessed 3 Mar 2023).

[10] https://www.w3.org/TR/vc-data-model. Accessed 8 Mar 2023.

- Pseudonymisation of personal data [s. GDPR Art 4(5)]
- Storing personal data available in a structured, commonly machine-readable format
- Enabling data subjects to intervene in the processing, providing information about the storage of personal data
- Having malware detection systems
- Training employees about basic "cyber hygiene"
- Establishing privacy and information security management systems, obligating processors contractually to implement specific data minimisation practices, etc.

A further challenge for practitioners is the gap between data protection requirements and systems development. In the next chapter, we explain some strategies to confront this problem.

4.3 Summary

- In the contexts of e-governments and from a usable privacy and security perspective, it is important to consider the centrality of OPS users as sovereign digital citizens over their personal data.
- From a citizens' perspective as users of OPS and data subjects, digital sovereignty refers to their confidence in controlling, using and understanding digital facilities.
- Citizens' digital sovereignty in the context of OPS requires mutual awareness and dialog between the state, the designers of online public services and citizens about forms of adoption and acceptance of digital services as well as about the needs and responsibilities of the involved actors in the implementation and in data privacy and security.
- To achieve digital sovereignty in the usage of OPSs in relation to data privacy and security, citizens need to be aware of the existence of OPSs' legal and technical aspects. As digital sovereign citizens in control over their personal data, they need to understand these legal and technical aspects of data privacy and security and be able to act consequently.
- For designers of OPS, responsibilities have also grown in relation to digital sovereignty. They must apply the concepts of data privacy by design and by default already acknowledged in GDPR Art 25 (s. Chap. 3) and use clear and plain language to provide information about data privacy and security.
- The challenges of OPS design related to data privacy include the need to consider OPS platform design for all citizens, public servants and enterprises; the need to include information about the benefits and risks of digital identities for all citizens, public servants and enterprises; and the need to design digital identity systems and platforms for all citizens, public servants and enterprises.
- From a usable privacy and security perspective, the challenges of developing OPS for all citizens begin with the design of access channels to public services on

the internet. The next challenge is the management of the digital identities and attributes to access the OPS on the internet.

- An early inclusion of citizens and public servants in the development of this new digital identity management method is necessary to avoid repeating the failures of the eID under the previous eIDAS (s. Chap. 2).
- Data protection by design or privacy by design (PbD) refers to the steps included in the design of a software product, services or processes concentrated on the maintenance or preservation of the highest privacy standards.
- An important aspect to build convergences in the practices and perspectives of the different groups involved in conceiving privacy by design in OPS is the definition of the end-users and the clear understanding of privacy and security responsibilities.
- A common challenge—particularly in light of the coming implementation of the single digital gateway and further for EUDI Wallet establishment in the EU—is the concretisation of data security measures for the multinational case as well as for single countries in the design of OPSs.

4.4 Examples and Exercises

4.4.1 Examples

An example of the acceptance of a decentralised identity wallet is available at Korir et al. (2022).

An example of a secure and privacy-preserving usage of machine learning in the area of health is available at Kaissis et al. (2020).

4.4.2 Exercises: Can You Explain? (Check Yourself)

1. What are central usability issues in ensuring the digital sovereignty of citizens in the context of OPS?
2. To achieve digital sovereignty when using OPS, it is essential to cover the needs of users. Name such needs.
3. Define seven classification categories of privacy and security principles.

Glossary

Data Privacy by Design "The use of pseudonymisation (replacing personally identifiable material with artificial identifiers) and encryption (encoding messages so only those authorised can read them)" [https://commission.europa.eu/law/

law-topic/data-protection/reform/rules-business-and-organisations/obligations/
what-does-data-protection-design-and-default-mean_en (accessed 8 Mar 2023)].

Data Privacy by Default "A social media platform should be encouraged to set users' profile settings in the most privacy-friendly setting by, for example, limiting from the start the accessibility of the users' profile so that it isn't accessible by default to an indefinite number of persons" [https://commission. europa.eu/law/law-topic/data-protection/reform/rules-business-and-organisa tions/obligations/what-does-data-protection-design-and-default-mean_en (accessed 8 Mar 2023)].

European Data Protection Board (EDPB) "The EDPB is an independent body at the European level with its own legal personality. It ensures, first and foremost, the consistent application of data protection rules throughout the European Union (EU)" [https://www.bfdi.bund.de/EN/Fachthemen/Gremienarbeit/ EuropaeischerDatenschutzausschuss/europaeischerdatenschutzausschuss_node. html (accessed 8 Mar 2023)].

Further Reading

Cavoukian A (2012) Privacy by design. IEEE Technol Soc Mag 31:18–19
EDPB (2020) Guidelines 4/2019 on Article 25 Data Protection by Design and by Default Version 2.0. Adopted on 20 October 2020
Floridi L (2020) The fight for digital sovereignty: what it is, and why it matters, especially for the EU. Philos Technol 33(3):369–378
https://www.w3.org/WAI/WCAG21/quickref/. Accessed 9 Mar 2023
https://www.w3.org/TR/vc-data-model. Accessed 8 Mar 2023

References

BMWi (Bundesministerium für Wirtschaft und Energie) (2021) Digitale Souveränität Bestandsaufnahme und Handlungsfelder. BMWi and ZEW Mannheim
Carretero S, Vuorikari R, Punie Y (2017) DigComp 2.1: The Digital Competence Framework for Citizens with eight proficiency levels and examples of use, EUR 28558 EN. https://doi.org/10. 2760/38842
Cavoukian A (2010a) Privacy by design: the 7 foundational principles: implementation and mapping of fair information practices. Information & Privacy Commissioner of Ontario, Toronto
Cavoukian A (2010b) Smart meters in Europe: Privacy by Design at its best. www. privacybydesign.com, April 2012. http://www.ipc.on.ca/images/Resources/pbd-smartmeters-europe.pdf. Accessed 23 Jan 2023
Cavoukian A (2012) Privacy by design. IEEE Technol Soc Mag 31:18–19
Couture S (2020) The diverse meanings of digital sovereignty. http://globalmedia.mit.edu/2020/0 8/05/the-diverse-meanings-of-digital-sovereignty/. Accessed 22 June 2022
Couture S, Toupin S (2019) What does the notion of 'sovereignty' mean when referring to the digital? New Media Soc 21(10):2305–2322

EDPB (2020) Guidelines 4/2019 on Article 25 Data Protection by Design and by Default Version 2.0. Adopted on 20 October 2020. https://edpb.europa.eu/sites/default/files/files/file1/edpb_guidelines_201904_dataprotection_by_design_and_by_default_v2.0_en.pdf.   Accessed 4 Jan 2023

EU (2023) https://www.europarl.europa.eu/RegData/etudes/BRIE/2023/740222/EPRS_BRI(2023) 740222_EN.pdf

Floridi L (2020) The fight for digital sovereignty: what it is, and why it matters, especially for the EU. Philos Technol 33(3):369–378

Gürses S, Troncoso C, Diaz C (2011) Engineering: privacy by design. Science 317(5842)

Gürses S, del Alamo JM (2016) Privacy engineering: shaping an emerging field of research and practice. IEEE Secur Privacy 14(2)

Halunen K (2020) Usable security & privacy methods and recommendations. https://pape.science/files/publications/CS4E20D3.5.pdf. Accessed 27 Jan 2023

Kaissis GA, Makowski MR, Rückert D et al (2020) Secure, privacy-preserving and federated machine learning in medical imaging. Nat Mach Intell 2:305–311. https://doi.org/10.1038/s42256-020-0186-1

Korir M, Parkin S, Dunphy P (2022) An empirical study of a decentralized identity wallet: usability, security, and perspectives on user control. In: Proceedings of the Eighteenth Symposium on Usable Privacy and Security (SOUPS 2022). pp 195–211

Kostova B, Gürses S, Troncoso C (2020) Privacy engineering meets software engineering. On the challenges of engineering privacy by design. https://arxiv.org/pdf/2007.08613.pdf. Accessed 23 Jan 2023

Lennartsson M, Kävrestad J, Nohlberg M (2021) Exploring the meaning of usable security – a literature review. Inf Comput Secur 29(4):647–663. https://doi.org/10.1108/ICS-10-2020-0167

Müller J, Tischer M, Thumel M et al (2022) Unboxing digitale Souveränität. Ein Scoping Review zu digitaler Souveränität von Individuen. Medienimpulse 60(4):1–37

Multimukwe C, Kolkowska E, Grönlund A (2019) Information privacy practices in e-government in an African least developing country, Rwanda. Electr J Inf Sys Dev Countries 85:2

Nurgalieva L, Frik A, Doherty G (2021) WiP: Factors affecting the implementation of privacy and security practices in software development: a narrative review. In: HoTSoS'21: 8th Annual Hot Topics in the Science of Security (HoTSoS) Symposium, April 13–15, 2021. ACM, New York, NY., 15 pp. https://doi.org/10.1145/1122445.1122456

Pohle J (2020) Digital Sovereignty. A new key concept of digital policy in Germany and Europe. Konrad Adenauer Stiftung, Bonn

Rodríguez-Hevía LF, Rodríguez-Fernández L, Ruiz-Gómez LR (2022) European regional inequalities in citizens' digital interaction with government. Emerald Insight. Transforming Government: People, Process and Policy 16(4):504–518

Schaub F, Cranor LF (2020) Usable and useful privacy interfaces. In: Breaux TD (ed) An introduction to privacy for technology professionals. IAPP

Venkatesh V, Hoehle H, Aljafari R (2014) A usability evaluation of the Obamacare website. Gov Inf Quart 31(4):669–680

Wissenschaftliche Arbeitsgruppe Nationaler Cyber-Sicherheitsrat (2022) Sichere digitale Identitäten. Impulspapier Juni 2022. https://www.forschung-it-sicherheit-kommunikationssysteme.de/dateien/forschung/2022-06-impulspapier-sichere-digitale-identitaeten.pdf. Accessed 15 Jul 2023

Chapter 5
Methods for Implementing Usable Secure Online Public Services

This chapter focuses on the methods of usable privacy and security that are more adequate for the design, development and evaluation of online public services. One central methodological approach is the inclusion of users' participation in the design and development of the interfaces. User participation in the usable security methods of online public services is crucial and vital to ensure that interfaces successfully support digital sovereignty and can be easily learned and implemented. User participation will help to improve and enhance performance and to increase user acceptance as well as citizens' trust in e-government. The chapter covers different techniques to ensure user participation in decision-making and actions during the system development process. It includes explanations of why, how and when we need to involve participants in the design process. Usable privacy and security methods for developing online public services combine quantitative and qualitative approaches. The chapter also explains what techniques are more appropriate for developing different specific online public services and how both methods can be combined.

5.1 Usable Privacy and Security Methods and the Design of OPS

A departing point for the design, development and evaluation of OPS from the perspective of usable privacy and security can be the data lifecycle in the OPS: data collection, data processing, data retention and data deletion. All these phases of the data lifecycle should be supported by privacy and security tools aiding compliance with the privacy principles and rights commented on in the previous chapters and meeting users' (data subjects') needs and understandings. Figure 5.1 shows an overview of usable privacy and security tools to apply for achieving basic data privacy rights.

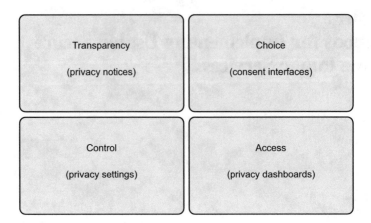

Fig. 5.1 Data subjects' privacy rights and related tools

Usable privacy and security methods are applied to address the data subjects' privacy rights in the design and implementation of privacy notices, consent interfaces, privacy settings and privacy dashboards. Common usability issues of privacy interfaces (i.e. conflating compliance and users' needs, lack of meaningful choices, poor integration of user experience, poor discoverability of privacy choices and security risk notices and confusing interfaces) should also be avoided when applying these methods. Privacy methods are based on privacy design principles (user centricity, relevance, understanding, actionability and integration). For OPS, these principles are specifically adapted to the contexts of use discussed in Chap. 2.

Qualitative techniques are applied to directly understand users'/stakeholders' perspectives and needs (Rohrer 2014). Quantitative techniques aim to measure concrete defined aspects. Capturing users'/stakeholders' perspectives and needs with qualitative techniques is based on researchers' interpretations of users'/stakeholders' narratives (i.e. recorded in semi-structured or open interviews). Qualitative techniques are commonly applied in the first phases of the data privacy design process. In the evaluation of data privacy and security tools, qualitative techniques are also applied, although at this stage, quantitative techniques are commonly used to measure the extent to which the users'/stakeholders' needs are met. Due to the interpretative nature of qualitative techniques focused on understanding users/stakeholders, the samples to apply these techniques are small and not representative. Quantitative techniques aim to measure defined features and may use representative samples. Both techniques can also be combined along the design process as mutually complementary tools that approach the users'/stakeholders' needs and the expected quality of the tools from different angles.

While privacy and security methods are applied along the whole OPS development process (design, implementation and evaluation), there are specific privacy design processes. These privacy design processes comprise six main steps, as shown in Fig. 5.2:

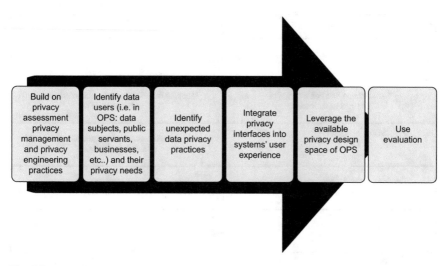

Fig. 5.2 Data privacy design process (based on Schaub and Cranor 2020)

In the first step, privacy assessments as well as privacy management and engineering practices are applied. Privacy impact assessments (PIAs)[1] are similar to user experience research (UX) but with different focuses (user experiences, data privacy) (Schaub and Cranor 2020). In the EU, the PIA was introduced in GDPR Art. 35.[2] At the same time, user centricity is also important in the GDPR, as we previously commented. In the context of OPS, usable privacy and security methods can benefit from the overlaps between PIA and UX, as shown in Fig. 5.3 based on Schaub and Cranor's (2020) explanations. Planning and identifying specific user groups/stakeholders are necessary for both PIA and UX. In the case of OPS, this includes mapping out the information flows between the data subjects or citizens eligible for the public services and using them on the internet as well as business and public administrations and service providers (see Chap. 4) and their concrete data privacy needs. Both PIA and UX are also iterative approaches to enable possible corrections in the starting definitions and concepts after applying assessment or research.

Common qualitative and quantitative techniques in these areas are semistructured interviews, diary studies, surveys, etc. To concretise and make the results of these techniques operational in further data privacy process phases, further techniques are used: personas, scenarios, user journeys, affinity diagrams, etc. Based on the research findings, the requirements for the concrete data privacy user experience design are defined. This includes the specification of users'/stakeholders'

---

[1] Guidelines for privacy impact assessment and data protection impact assessment can be consulted in ISO/IEC 29134/2017: https://www.iso.org/obp/ui/#iso:std:iso-iec:29134:ed-1:v1:en. Accessed 7 Feb 2023.

The Guidelines of the European Data Protection Impact Assessment (EDPIA): https://ec.europa.eu/newsroom/article29/items/611236. Accessed 7 Feb 2023.

[2] https://gdpr-info.eu/issues/privacy-impact-assessment/. Accessed 7 Feb 2023.

PIA	UX research
Planning	
Identification and consultation of relevant stakeholders	Mapping out user journeys and interactions with a system
	Identification and consultation of relevant stakeholders
Provides recommendations for mitigating privacy risks	Produces design requirements to meet user needs and mitigate usability issues
Iterations	

Fig. 5.3 Similarities between privacy impact assessment (PIA) and user experience (UX) research (based on Schaub and Cranor 2020)

data privacy and security needs and goals. The definition of concrete metrics is also important at this stage. Potential contradictions between users'/stakeholders' needs, regulation requirements or costs must also be considered in these metrics. Based on the results of the PIA/UX research, the design of data privacy and security tools (s. Fig. 5.3) using, among others, nudging methods begins, followed by the evaluation phase.

To understand and better integrate the needs of users/stakeholders in data privacy and security tools, usable privacy and security methods use participative techniques. Design thinking is one of the most commonly used participative techniques and is increasingly used for OPS design, although it is not commonly applied in usable privacy and security. Because of their potential importance to include citizens in the design and implementation of usable secure OPS, we first focus in the next section on the participative approaches for designing usable private and secure OPS before explaining the use of nudging in usable privacy and security and the evaluation methods included in the data privacy design process.

5.1.1 Participative Approaches for the Design of Usable Secure OPS

A common approach applied for the design of usable secure OPS is design thinking. Design thinking methods are based on the ideas of participatory design (Sanoff 2006), user-centred design (Norman 1988), service design (Kimbell 2010) and human-centred design (Gasson 2003), which confront the increasing integration and complexity of technological products and services in everyday life and the

1. Discover	2. Interpret	3. Create	4. Experiment	5. Evolve
I have a challenge.	I learned something.	I see an opportunity.	I have an idea.	I tried something new.
How do I approach it?	How do I interpret it?	How do I create?	How do I build it?	How do I evolve it?
1.1 Understand the challenge	2.1 Tell **stories**	3.1 Generate **ideas**	4.1 Make **prototypes**	5.1 Track learnings
1.2 Conduct research	2.2 Search for **meaning**	2.2 Refine ideas	4.2 Get feedback	5.2 Move forward
1.3 Gather inspiration	2.3 Frame opportunities			

Fig. 5.4 Design thinking process. Adapted from the following: https://education.uky.edu/nxgla/wp-content/uploads/sites/33/2016/11/Design-Thinking-for-Educators.pdf (p. 15). Accessed 1 Jul 2022

consequences of the disconnections between cultures and artefacts in the process of technological development.

In the public management-oriented literature, design thinking is conceptualised as an organisational resource to develop and manage innovation (Kimbell 2011; Brown 2008; Johansson-Sköldberg et al. 2013). Design thinking basically implements different development methods such as ethnographic and visual techniques as well as modelling or prototyping (Bason 2010). In addition, finding needs, brainstorming and designing are among the common procedures of design thinking (Seidel and Fixson 2013: 19). Several principles guide the implementation of design thinking methods: user focus, problem contextualisation, visualisation, diversity and experimentation (Carlgren et al. 2016). User focus refers to the inclusion of users in the development process of final products. This is done through the use of qualitative research methods and participatory approaches such as focus groups. Through user focus, the needs and desires of users are better understood, and the designed products are optimised. The principle of problem contextualisation also guides the optimisation of the designed products in that the spaces in which users interact with the products and with other users are considered. The principle of visualisation refers to the presentation of product designs and their optimisations. Furthermore, diverse perspectives of different actors are cooperatively included in the design thinking process. This is what the principle of diversity refers to. Experimentation refers to the iterative approach that brings together user focus, visualisation and optimisation of product designs (Carlgren et al. 2016).

How the design thinking process is applied in practice is explained in the next paragraphs: *design thinking in practice*.

Design thinking is implemented iteratively in different phases. Figure 5.4 shows the five common phases of design thinking processes. Although these five phases (discovering or understanding the problem and users, interpreting the problem and

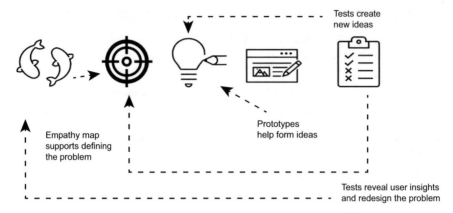

Fig. 5.5 Iterative design thinking process. Adapted from the following: https://www.interaction-design.org/literature/article/5-stages-in-the-design-thinking-process. Accessed 19 Jun 2022

user behaviour, generating ideas, experimenting with prototypes and developing or testing and improving) are basically present in design thinking processes, there are some nuances in the literature about the concepts' differences involved.[3]

First, an attempt is made to understand the problem or challenge that is to be solved. A common feature to consider is that the different phases do not follow each other in a linear fashion. Figure 5.5 shows an overview of the iterative practice of this first process phase.

The five phases or aspects of the design thinking process are to be understood as iterative activities rather than linear sequences. This is one of the advantages of the design thinking approach: the information in the different process phases can contribute to the refinement and revision of the problem definition at any time.

Before the first phase, the teams are organised, and the rooms and materials are prepared. The ideal number of team participants is 2–5. Additional people can be invited for the brainstorming sessions. However, for decision-making on interpretations of the problem, refinement of ideas and the experimentation phase, it is better to keep a small group of a maximum of five people.

For the definition of the group, it is important that people from diverse perspectives are integrated into the group. The integration of diverse perspectives of the group participants should help to represent the target group as much as possible. Furthermore, it is helpful to assign roles to the group participants. These roles (e.g. leader, coordinator, motivator, etc.) should be adapted to the characteristics of the participants to achieve a productive group dynamic. In addition to the interactions of the group participants in the different work phases, individual "thinking spaces" should also be provided.

---

[3] See https://web.archive.org/web/20210411035401/https://experience.sap.com/skillup/introduction-to-design-thinking/ (accessed 3 Jun 2022).

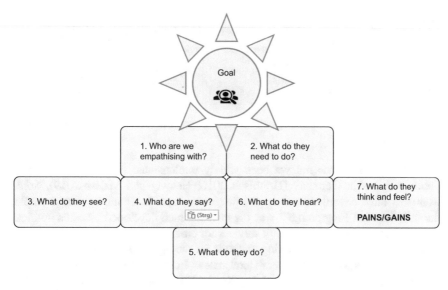

Fig. 5.6 Elements of an empathy map. Adapted from the following: https://medium.com/the-xplane-collection/updated-empathy-map-canvas-46df22df3c8a. Accessed 23 Jun 2022

In the first phases of the design thinking process, the creation of an empathic relationship with the target group should be supported. It is expected that the defined problem is understood empathically in the context of customers. To support the creation of an empathic understanding of the customer's problem, so-called empathy maps can be used. Figure 5.6 shows an example of the categories that can be used for this. The empathy map was developed by Dave Grey. The method of using this 4map aims to better assess the customers of a product and understand their needs and emotions in relation to purchase decisions or product experiences. First, a specific question is asked about the customer's emotions, i.e. "Why should I use service x?". Then, the question is asked about who we empathise with, followed by further questions about the different aspects related to the person's experience with the service (What should the person do? What does she/he see, say, do and hear regarding the service?)

After the discovery with the help of empathy maps and the interpretation phase, in which the designer group with people with diverse perspectives on the design thinking output is established, the third design thinking phase takes place (Fig. 5.4). In this third phase of the design thinking process, the focus is on dialogue versus debate. Instead of considering problem definitions as fixed constructs, self-evident facts are questioned in the design group and debated in a solution-oriented way. It is important during these dialogues and debates to apply a guiding methodology that supports the avoidance of unproductive discussions. Simple design thinking approaches such as structuring the dialogues and using post-it cards to note individual ideas before discussing them in the group can be very helpful at this stage (Liedka and Salzan 2019).

Action Learning	Network mapping	Journey mapping	Reflexive practice
Solutions developed considering the problems' context	Interventions delivered through network arrangements	To understand citizens' and stakeholders' service journeys, challenges, aspirations	Plan codesigning to identify barriers

Fig. 5.7 Learning tools to codesign public services. Adapted from the following: Evans and Terrey (2016: 248)

Design thinking has not yet been widely implemented for the digitisation of public services in Germany (Dribbisch 2016; Heuwig and Maletz 2019). Some examples have nevertheless emerged in recent years. In Hamburg, for example, the "Digital First Programme"[4] was organised, which developed asbestos notifications and residents' parking permit services for citizens and businesses using design thinking methods. Design thinking methods for the digitalisation of public services are also increasingly used in other federal states.[5] In Munich, a so-called Global Gov Jam was organised at the city administration in 2017.[6] Originally, the concept of the Global Gov Jam was developed in Australia.[7] People who are interested in developing public services meet for 48 h over a weekend to realise prototypes together.

5.1.2   Participative Methods for Implementing Usable Public Services

In addition to the application of design thinking methods in the design of OPS, other participative approaches are implemented as well. For example, codesign processes include several techniques (action learning, network mapping, journey mapping, reflexive practice) (Evans and Terrey 2016) (see Fig. 5.7). The "action learning" method refers to the idea that solutions to problems can only be solved in the context in which the problem arose. "Network mapping" focuses on analysing the networks that are part of the problem context. Journey mapping is used to understand the challenges and pathways that confront users. Furthermore, the products or services are developed cooperatively to establish a reflexive practice in the process. This so-called reflexive practice aims to develop a plan to confront possible barriers associated with the product or service.

---

[4] See https://www.bva.bund.de/SharedDocs/Downloads/DE/Presse/Interviews/Fachmedien/vitako_verwaltung_agile_entwicklung.pdf?__blob=publicationFile&v=2 (accessed 10 Oct 2022).

[5] See https://muenchen.digital/blog/jung-modern-agil-design-thinking-in-der-verwaltung/ (accessed 10 Oct 2022).

[6] See both https://muenchen.digital/blog/govjam-2017-design-von-verwaltungsservices/ and https://www.davidfreudenthal.com/portfolio/govjam/ (accessed 10 Oct 2022).

[7] http://globaljams.org/jam/globalgovjam. Accessed 10 Oct 2022.

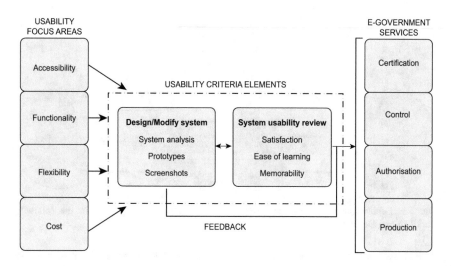

Fig. 5.8 Integration of usability in the design of public services. Adapted from the following: Mayoka and Humpfrey (2016: 8)

For the implementation of public services, these participative design methods enable the contextualisation of public services, the structured experimentation of policies, the generation of evidence from implementation practice and the sharing of the risks of potential failures in the implementation of policies or public services between citizens and stakeholders (Evans and Terrey 2016).

Design thinking methods can be used to increase the usability or usable security of e-government services such as user accounts together with citizens. Figure 5.8 shows a theoretical framework for the implementation of usability in e-government services. Mayoka and Humpfrey (2016) show the importance of four usability aspects for the development of e-government services: accessibility, functionality, flexibility and cost. These aspects should be tested with citizens in prototypes. Other authors have considered and empirically investigated further aspects. Verkijika and De Wet (2018) draw on public values theories (Cordella and Bonina 2012; UN DESA 2020) to investigate six fundamental aspects of e-government web page usability or quality: accessibility, citizen engagement, trust development, responsiveness, dialogue and quality of information and services.

Figure 5.9 shows the specific perspective of implementing public values ideas in the development of e-government websites that Verkijika and De Wet (2018) apply. The experiences of users are the starting point for the development of web pages. In particular, the aspect of establishing trust, which Verkijika and De Wet (2018) consider in their research, includes the dimension of data protection and data security. Data protection and security decisively influence the trust dimension of the development and implementation of e-government websites, as has been empirically shown (Alsaghier and Hussain 2012; Alzahrani et al. 2016).

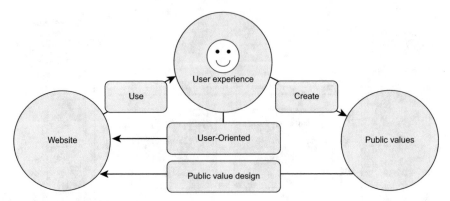

Fig. 5.9 Public values perspective of e-government websites. Adapted from the following: Verkijika and De Wet (2018: 3)

Beyond participative methods for implementing usable secure OPS, also called the Usable Security by Design approach in human-centred design (Payne and Edwards 2008), the application of nudging methods aims to change users' behaviour to enhance data privacy and security protection. The application of nudging methods is controversial due to the asymmetrical positions between users and developers in the implementation of OPS data privacy and security. Specific privacy nudges called privacy-enhancing technologies (PETs) have already been established, for instance, in private companies, to comply with data protection laws. The European Commission has also promoted the use of PETs for data protection.[8] While PETs have been criticised for their manipulative intentions,[9] the negative extremes of PETs are the so-called dark patterns or sludges.

In contrast to these negatively manipulative nudging methods, the so-called transparency-enhancing technologies (TETs) emphasise the transparency aspect of usable privacy and security and particularly transparency, as it is included in the data privacy laws (i.e. GDPR) to build instruments that aim to support digital sovereignty. In the next section, we explain these nudging methods in usable privacy to explain how to address the challenges of data privacy in OPS with TETs.

---

[8] https://eur-lex.europa.eu/EN/legal-content/summary/promoting-data-protection-by-privacy-enhancing-technologies.html. Accessed 6 Jan 2023.

[9] See, for example, https://www.adalovelaceinstitute.org/blog/privacy-enhancing-technologies-not-always-our-friends/. Accessed 6 Jan 2023.

5.1.3   Intervention Methods of Usable Privacy and Security Implementation: Nudging

In addition to participatory approaches of usable privacy and security in the design OPS, nudging methods basically aim to change users' data privacy behaviour towards already implemented IT services on the internet. Questions associated with nudging are, for example, whether it is legitimate to nudge at all, with which means and by whom (Acquisti et al. 2017). Based on nudging principles, privacy-enhancing technologies (PETs)[10] are technologies aiming to change users' behaviours to protect data privacy and security, particularly the confidentiality dimension of data security. PET is applied by governments but also by private companies seeking profit and actors with questionable ethical intentions. The negative side of nudging is called dark patterns or sludges.

Dark patterns were defined as tools used in internet websites and apps to induce users to perform online activities unconsciously or unintentionally (e.g. accepting cookies and certain privacy settings) (Brignull 2013). Dark patterns were later categorised as follows (Mathur et al. 2021): user interface characteristics; impact mechanisms on users, divided into 13 different impact modalities; the role of user interface designers; and benefits and harms of dark patterns. Other authors do not differentiate between different dark pattern categories. They focus on the harm done to users by the implementation of dark patterns (Zagal et al. 2013; Gray et al. 2018; Waldman 2020).

Another term associated with the negative side of nudging is "sludges". Sludges are considered the radical opposite of nudges. While nudges are placed on the "good side" of digital tools for influencing behaviour because of their potential positive behavioural impacts, sludges occupy all negative interpretations of the term (Thaler 2018; Ip et al. 2018; Sunstein 2019, 2020). This radical dichotomisation of nudges vs. sludges has recently been challenged (Mills 2020). Mills (2020) proposes a taxonomy of nudges and sludges that shows disagreements between the two and their tolerance and intolerance in different areas.

Mill's (2020) taxonomy (Fig. 5.10) is based on the cognitive, emotional and physical factors proposed by Kahneman (2011) that influence individual willingness to volunteer. For example, economic incentives are considered in nudge theories as desirable "disutilities" (frictions), while hedonistic (changing desirable aspects to influence decisions), social (changing social or moral costs to influence decisions) or "dark" (obscurantist) (changing psychological or cognitive effort to influence decisions) incentives are not. These factors are examples of sludges but also aspects of nudging in general (Mills 2020: 8).

Both nudges and sludges use incentives to change behaviour. From this perspective, they are symmetrical. The difference between the two is in the direction in

---

[10] Pelkola (2012) distinguishes six different types of PETs: system security access, data encryption, authorisation on the basis of defined user profiles, data separation, data anonymisation and biometric authentication.

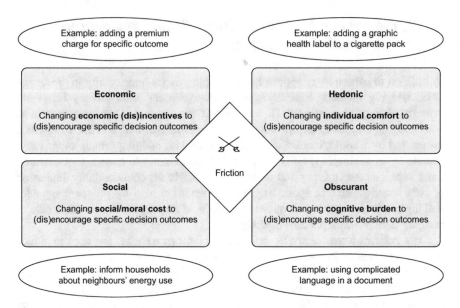

Fig. 5.10 "Frictions", discordances between nudges and sludges. Based on the following: Mills (2020: 7)

which they intend to direct behaviour. To differentiate between the two symmetrical aspects, Mills (2020) proposes to consider the changes in the design of options (choice architecture) building on the ideas of Wendel (2016) in the context of digital design. Wendel (2016) claims that all design is implicitly persuasive. This means that the design of options (choice architecture) is always unavoidable.

According to Wendel (2016), interventions should be evaluated considering the following criteria: what was developed as part of the intervention, how were these developments implemented and what behaviour was expected as a result. Mills (2020) also uses the concept of a "Pareto intervention" to identify possible biases in nudges regarding their unilateral beneficial consequences for certain groups. Pareto interventions are those in which the designers of options (choice architects) can increase their own advantage by maximising the benefits from the intervention. This means that the benefits are not only for one actor involved but also for the decision-makers of the interventions and the target groups. Furthermore, the concept of "rent-seeking intervention" refers to the situation where designers (choice architects) can extract the maximum of their own benefits from the intervention without producing benefits for the decision-makers (Mills 2020: 14).

Nudges and sludges are not considered in this classification as implicitly or per se good or bad forms of intervention but rather as instances of change in disfavour of nudging ("frictions"). Frictions of nudging were listed by Gunawan et al. (2021) to provide an overview of the most common negative patterns of nudging. These are no consent checkbox, no account deletion, no privacy settings, notification setting opt-in by default, visual option precedence, no bulk options for settings, general

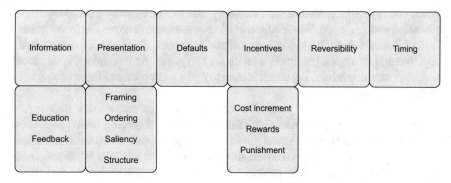

Fig. 5.11 Nudging method dimensions in usable data privacy and security. Based on Acquisti et al. (2017: 13)

pop-up nags, privacy setting opt-in by default, extraneous notification badges and account required.

Gunawan et al. (2021) found in their comparative study of mobile apps, mobile browsers and web browser versions of 150 services that many dark patterns vary by platform. The most commonly used modality of dark patterns is the lack of a consent checkbox for privacy policy.

In the context of online public services, Utz et al. (2019) found in a random sample of 1000 consent notes from the 500 most popular EU websites that some visual manipulative element was used in 57.4% of cases. For example, websites more often use particularly eye-catching colours to draw attention to unfriendly preset ("defaults") privacy measures (Gov.UK 2022).

Nudging and the avoidance of "dark patterns" and "sludges" are especially significant in political areas or in the design of public online services because online public services should be fully accessible and understandable for all citizens, as we explained in previous chapters. Alemanno and Spina (2014: 438) call policy-makers who use nudging "architects of choice" who prepare contexts, processes, content and the decision-making structure and its environment (Piasecki 2017). In this context, Piasecki (2017) raises the question of the legitimacy of these so-called architects of choice vis-à-vis society. Enhancing citizens' digital decision skills and the development of usability tools combined with participatory approaches are some ways to confront the choices dilemmas in the architecture of data privacy and security of OPS.

In usable privacy and security, nudging methods are used to confront biases and heuristics as well as incomplete and asymmetric information: information, presentation with contextual cues, defaults to reduce user effort in system configurations, incentives to motivate users to behave consistently with their preferences, error reversibility and timing or determining the right moment to nudge (Acquisti et al. 2017); see Fig. 5.11. The use of nudging as information transfer aims to eliminate the negative effects of asymmetric information and overestimation of one's own knowledge about the consequences of privacy interventions. Effective nudging should be clear and brief and only need to include relevant messages (Acquisti et al. 2017: 13).

When conveying information with nudging, two subdimensions are distinguished: education and feedback. While educational information influences the future behaviour of users before they confront certain activities, feedback is continuously implemented through all interactions with the IT system. An example of educational nudges is nutrition labels. Feedback is used to make users aware of the consequences of their behaviour.

In the context of data protection and IT security, educational nudges are implemented to support users in their decisions regarding data protection (e.g. when granting rights in social media). The improvement of educational notices by keeping the information provided short and understandable, as is the case with nutrition labels or standardised privacy labels (Schaub et al. 2015; Kelley et al. 2010, cited in Acquisti et al. 2017: 14), is also suggested as a nudging strategy to avoid the users' usual avoidance of reading data protection and security information ("overwhelming notices") (Acquisti et al. 2017).

Regarding the presentation of data privacy and security information, four subdimensions are distinguished: framing, ordering, salience and structure. Framing refers to the presentation of the consequences of privacy options. For example, certain risks are presented in an exaggerated form to keep users away from risky actions. For example, visual signals are used in car traffic situations to avoid speeding. These measures affect the self-assessment of drivers, so the effects of the transfer of use in other areas of life are not immediate (Acquisti et al. 2017).

In addition to the ordering and saliency of specific options when presenting information about data privacy and security, the structure (e.g. with filters or search support) subdimension of information presentation tries to classify options to help users to overview privacy and security options.

In the field of usable privacy and security, several studies have shown the effects of applying these nudging dimensions (form of information presentation, relevance, structure). Braunstein et al. (2011) found in their study that the wording of the privacy configuration questions or a reminder of the sensitivity of the data influenced users' behaviour in that they were less willing to share private data. Brandimarte et al. (2013) also found that when users overestimate their self-assessment of their knowledge about privacy risks, they are more willing to share private data than when they do not overestimate their knowledge. Paradoxically, participants in the study were more willing to share private data when they were informed about privacy risks than when they were not exposed to this information. These research results show how important it is not to generalise information provision but to design it in the context of self-assessment of user knowledge about privacy risks.

With respect to the relevance of information intermediaries, research by Bravo-Lillo et al. (2013) shows that users avoid downloading dubious software when the information about the software intermediaries is placed at the forefront of the information. Examples of usable data privacy and security nudges that help structure privacy information by Mazzia et al. (2012), Gao et al. (2012) and Albergotti (2014) show the positive effects of visualisations with relevant or simplified information on privacy (Acquisti et al. 2017: 20).

Another dimension of nudging in usable privacy and security is so-called default nudging. Default nudges prescribe how users' private data are protected and shared. This dimension aims to change users' common attitude of not changing the default options of internet applications (Acquisti et al. 2017:21). There are different forms of default nudging. Goldstein et al. (2008) distinguish between general default nudges and those that are personalised, requiring information about the user. Some examples of default nudges are autocompletion tools and restrictive default privacy setting tools that lead users to share less information (Iaonnu et al. 2021).

The dimension of nudging with incentives involves the implementation of penalties or rewards. In the area of "usable privacy and security", for example, nudges are used that introduce costs (e.g. time costs) for the use or activation of data protection measures. Grossklags and Acquisti (2007) found in their study that the price users are willing to pay for selling their private data is higher than the price they would accept for protecting their data (Acquisti et al. 2017: 22).

To reduce the effects of errors, nudges of the error reversibility dimension are implemented. One example is the "undo" function when sharing private pictures on social media. Users are given the opportunity to revise their decision about sharing private data. Timing, or the specific moments when the usable privacy and security nudges are presented to users, is another nudging dimension.

In sum, while all these nudging dimensions have shown significant effects on information disclosure, applying incentives and default nudges (i.e. opting-out) or some presentation options, such as calls for action as well as combinations of several nudge dimensions, seem to be particularly effective (Iaonnu et al. 2021). On the other hand, Iaonnu et al. (2021) warn about using strategies to change behaviour by educating users, for example, with information nudges. Moreover, these authors point out that influencing users to increase the disclosure of information seems to be more effective than nudging to decrease disclosure. Another critical aspect of nudges is the lack of consideration of the digital divide.

These different solutions are to be transferred to the area of information brokerage regarding data protection and IT security and more concretely in the context of online public services.

While PETs as a nudging tool in usable privacy and security contribute to improving privacy, they may bring some problems. For example, decreased accountability, particularly in the context of OPS, is crucial and must be addressed through other means, for example, with TETs.

We explain this usable privacy aspect in the next paragraphs: *transparency-enhancing technologies (TETs)*.

Transparency-enhancing technologies (TETs) basically aim at reducing the information asymmetries between users and providers on the internet. According to Hansen (2008: 191), TETs are "tools which can provide to the individual concerned clear visibility of aspects relevant to [its personal] data and the individual's privacy" (Hansen 2008: 191 cit. by Zimmermann 2015: 1). Zimmermann (2015) explains that TETs can complement PETs by offering users insights into a data controller's intended and actual data handling behaviour. Zimmermann's classification of the numerous TETs existing on the internet (i.e. Google's "My Account", "Mozilla Privacy Icons") helps to understand the complementarity with PETs.

More recently, Murmann and Fischer-Hübner (2017) conducted a review of the literature about TETs. Murmann and Fischer-Hübner (2017) point out that data visualisation is frequently simplified with the intention of addressing an audience as diverse as the internet community. The price of these simplifications and abstractions is information loss and reduced interactional capabilities, leading to a compromise between the functionality of TETs and their usability. Common backgrounds for TETs are three main intersected and mutually dependent topics: privacy, transparency and usability (Murmann and Fischer-Hübner 2017). In contrast to PETs, TETs emphasise the transparency dimension of usable privacy and security. Transparency can be understood in connection to the definition in the GDPR. The concept of transparency in the GDPR is mainly covered in Chap. III, Art. 12 et seq.[11] As Murmann and Fischer-Hübner (2017) explain, transparency relates to the visualisation of deliberately or accidentally disclosed individual data items to a particular data controller or downstream processor. Transparency refers to the information about data processing that must be provided to the users (data subjects in the terminology of the GDPR). This information provided with clear and plain language must be concise, intelligible, transparent and easily accessible.

The transparency principle constitutes a basic requirement for processing operations because for data subjects, the provision of complete and accessible information is necessary to be able to make their data rights effective (Bieker 2022: 25). The data subjects can only be able to have insight into the scope of the disclosed data and to make informed decisions on their legal rights (i.e. rectification or deletion of her data (GDPR, Chap. III, Art. 16 et seq.)), if they have comprehensive knowledge of underlying processes, involved stakeholders and data flows (Murmann and Fischer-Hübner 2017). Transparency is therefore crucial in usable privacy and security. Because the GDPR's approach relies on a traditional consent-based framework, users depend on transparency to build their decisions (Hartzog 2018).

TETs can be classified into two groups: "ex ante" and "ex post". While "ex ante" TETs guide users' process of making decisions before making choices about disclosing any personal data to a data controller, "ex post" TETs visualise disclosed personal data to make transparent the processes underlying the whole data disclosure process. The process to be visualised begins at the moment that the users disclose their data (Murmann and Fischer-Hübner 2017). Murman and Fischer-Hübner (2017) point out in their review that most of the TET research has focused on ex ante TETs.

This TET classification uses the application time as a parameter. Zimmermann (2015) shows 11 other choices of classification parameters, including the execution environment, the data types presented, the targeted audience, the delivery mode, the authentication level (fully identified, pseudonymous, anonymous), the interactivity level, the scope, the assurance level, the transparency dimensions (collection,

---

[11] https://eur-lex.europa.eu/eli/reg/2016/679/oj. Accessed 2 Dec 2022.

analysis, usage, second usage), the attacker model and the information source. For OPS, it is important to account for these different parameters, but most of all, it is important to consider the authentication level and the transparency, aspects that we commented on in Chap. 3.

From the perspective of usable privacy and security, transparency is also a social, cultural and individual concept. Transparency is understood in this concept as going beyond the development of digital tools to support the provision of information about data privacy and security and to evaluate their efficacy. It means considering the meaning and sense of transparency in its social and cultural context where the legal institutionalisation of this concept makes sense and is enacted.[12] Emphasising the interdisciplinary character of usable privacy and security in the development of TETs, Trask et al. (2020) elaborate the concept of "structured transparency". As the authors point out, deficits of PETs regarding accountability could be circumvented by applying not only technological "solutions" but also a combination of technical, social and institutional approaches from different disciplines that they denominate "structural transparency". The five components of "structured transparency" are input and output privacy, input and output verification and flow governance. These five components correspond to common challenges in data privacy and security. Input privacy is related to the data subject's ability to process information that is hidden and to allow others to process the information without revealing their identity. Output privacy refers to the allowance of receiving or reading an information output without being able to infer further information about the input and, *symmetrically, to contribute to the input of an information flow without worrying that the later output could be reverse engineered to learn about your input* (Trask et al. 2020: 4). Input privacy aims at facilitating information flow while preventing identity leakage, whereas output privacy prevents reverse engineering of the input data.

Input verification allows us to verify that received information from an information flow is sourced from trusted entities, and (symmetrically), it allows us to send information such that the output can be verifiably associated with the source. Output verification allows us to verify the attributes of any computational information processing in an information flow. Flow governance is achieved once each party has the guarantee that the information flow will preserve the intended use. Open questions remain about what authority is allowed to modify the information flow (Trask et al. 2020).

The structured transparency concept does not cover three major technical problems in the development of TETs: the copy problem, the bundling problem and the recursive oversight problem.

---

[12]For a critical reflexion on transparency and e-government, see, for example, Bannister F and Connolly R (2011) The Trouble with Transparency: A Critical Review of Openness in e-Government. In. Policy & internet: 3 (1): 8. See https://onlinelibrary.wiley.com/doi/epdf/10.2202/1944-2866.1076?saml_referrer (accessed 5 Dec 2022).

The copy problem refers to the released governance of shared information to the recipient, who is free from technical limitations to misuse even if ex post legal or social sanctions exist. Data owners often confront a trade-off as a result when they have to decide to share information. Another related consequence is the bundling problem. This problem consists of the difficulty of sharing some information without revealing additional bits. This is because conventional encoding does not allow the sharing of individual bits or a bit is not able to be trusted or verified without contextualisation supported by other bits (Trask et al. 2020).

Trask et al. (2020) explain that although the inclusion of oversight from third-party institutions can solve issues caused by copy and bundling problems, a recursive oversight problem arises as a consequence. The third-party institutions overseeing the information are not necessarily bundled by other institutions controlling them. Trask et al. (2020) remark that it can be hard to hold those third-party institutions accountable.

These three problems restrict the practice of structured transparency conceived by Trask et al. (2020: 5) and lead to numerous data sharing dilemmas: *either useful-but-sensitive data goes unused or society has to absorb the costs of sharing information with misaligned actors*.

A combination of social, legal and technical tools contributes to resolving these problems. Trask et al. (2020) propose a classification of these solutions for structured transparency based on the five structured transparency components explained above (input and output privacy, input and output verification and flow governance). Some examples of these tools are for input privacy the development of cryptographic techniques and for output privacy the methods of differential privacy. Input verification tools use a combination of public key infrastructures with cryptographic signatures and zero knowledge proofs, among others. These tools can be combined with output verification tools to prevent the bundling problem. An example of techniques for the flow governance component is secure multiparty computing enabling the selection of arbitrary parties to govern the flow relying on cryptographic techniques to trust the system.

In the next paragraphs, we explain *visual TET techniques*. There are several techniques for elaborating TETs and reducing information asymmetries between governments and data subjects in OPSs. In recent years, scholars have emphasised the benefits of visual methods in usable privacy to overcome increasing obstacles to achieving transparency in data processing (i.e. Rossi and Lenzini 2020). Rossi and Lenzini (2020) summarise eight main obstacles to achieving transparency in data processing or, in other words, effective legal-technical communication: language complexity, vagueness of terms, wall of text (confusing display of information), excessive length, lack of audience-tailoring, bad timing, lack of familiarity and scattered information. Visual transparency design patterns aim to confront these obstacles. They can be classified into four categories (explanation, navigation, overview and emphasis) (Rossi and Lenzini 2020). The explanation category includes illustrations, frequently asked questions (FAQs), timelines, swimlanes and comics; the navigation category contains meaningful organisation and companion icons; the overview category comprises layered notices and videos; and the emphasis category includes highlighted texts and alert icons.

In the framework of the e-government and OPS, the usage of icons has been particularly encouraged to support the transparency of data processing in relation to the implementation of the GDPR. These techniques aim to facilitate the data subjects' identification of the processing of their data to enable a certain degree of control over this processing, as defined in the GDPR.

The creation and usage of icons to facilitate the understanding of privacy texts have existed for several years, but with limited success (Thouvenin et al. 2020). For example, in the position of the European Parliament adopted in 2014 regarding the processing of personal data and on the free movement of such data (GDPR),[13] several icons were suggested in relation to the implementation of GDPR Article 13a "Standardised information policies". Thouvenin et al. (2020) explain that the implementation of usable privacy icons fails because icon creators try to accomplish both self-explanation and depict the complexities of privacy issues at the same time. Aiming to overcome previous failures, Thouvenin et al. (2020) elaborate usable privacy icons without self-explanatory claims and consider that icons should complement each data privacy text rather than aiming at replacing their complexities. For that, these authors based upon three main ideas: First, the privacy icons should only depict the relevant content and not the entire privacy policy. Second, the relevance of the content should be assessed from the perspective of the data subjects. Third, privacy icons cover aspects of data processing that must be ensured by every data processor in any way. Nineteen privacy icons were developed and labelled based on these ideas.[14] They cover six topics: type of personal data, source of personal data, purpose of processing, special processing, disclosure to third parties and place of processing. The icons are accessible and usable as complementary materials to the GDPR text.

Another example of usable privacy techniques creating icons to achieve transparency in data processing according to the GDPR is the Data Protection as a Corporate Social Responsibility Framework (UM-DPCSR) research project at the European Centre on Privacy and Cybersecurity (ECPC).[15] As a result of several meetings with a group of data protection stakeholders, intergovernmental stakeholders and business stakeholders, the research team elaborated a set of icons related to Article 13 and 14 GDPR (Information Notice icons) as well as data protection icons for high-risk processing activities (Balboni and Francis 2022).

In a similar way, the project "Data Privacy Icons Set" (DaPIS)[16] also focused on usable privacy visualisation techniques to achieve data processing transparency. In

---

[13] https://eur-lex.europa.eu/legal-content/EN/TXT/HTML/?uri=CELEX:52014AP0212&from=DE (see Annex). Accessed 27 Feb 2023.

[14] The icons can be accessed in https://privacy-icons.ch (accessed 27 Feb 2023).

[15] See https://www.maastrichtuniversity.nl/sites/default/files/2022_03_16_um-dpcsr_framework_v3.3_balboni_francis.pdf (accessed 28 Feb 2023).

[16] http://gdprbydesign.cirsfid.unibo.it/dapis-the-data-protection-icon-set/. Accessed 27 Feb 2023.

the framework of this project, the researchers created 43 icons grouped into 6 topics (data types, legal bases, processing purposes, rights of the data subject, processing types, roles) based upon the transparency requirements defined in GDPR Article 12.8. The first step for the elaboration of the icons was the creation of an ontology of the GDPR enabling us to determine the relations between the legal concepts and to associate the semantics to the icons using metadata. In a series of design workshops, the researchers visualised the icons and then tested them in an iterative process. The last version of the icons corresponds to the fourth design iteration[17] (Rossi and Palmirani 2020).

All these usable privacy visual techniques may contribute to supporting data subjects' digital sovereignty. However, usable privacy and security in practice should go beyond the provision of understandable information towards the "actionability of this information" (Rossi and Lenzini 2020). Moreover, in the practice of OPS system development, data protection and security complexities may turn out to be overwhelming. Some scholars have elaborated techniques to confront this. We explain some of them in the next section.

5.1.4   Methods to Confront the Gaps Between Data Protection Requirements and Systems Development

TET methods can be helpful for OPS to achieve information transparency and trust between citizens and administrations and to support digital sovereignty. However, as we commented in the previous chapter, privacy by design is frequently difficult to establish due to the gap between data protection requirements (i.e. in the GDPR) and software and systems development practices (Colesky et al. 2016). A specific approach (Bano et al. 2017) elaborates several strategies and tactics to confront this gap. Figure 5.12 shows an overview of these strategies.

The four tactics can be understood as goals of the data privacy protection quality attributes, which are non-functional requirements such as performance, security and privacy. Hiding means making personal data unobservable or unlinkable. Associated tactics to hide personal data are restricting unauthorised access and mixing or processing personal data randomly to reduce correlation, encrypt, obfuscate and dissociate (removing the correlations between different parts of personal data). Minimising corresponds to the principle of limiting the processing of personal data included in the GDPR. There are four tactics associated with this strategy: excluding, selecting, stripping or destroying.

The separate strategy includes the tactics of distributing (partitioning of personal data) and isolating (processing parts of personal data independently without corre-lating or accessing the related parts). The abstract strategy focuses on limiting the amount of detail of the personal data that should be processed. For this, three tactics

---

[17] http://gdprbydesign.cirsfid.unibo.it/methodology/. Accessed 27 Feb 2023.

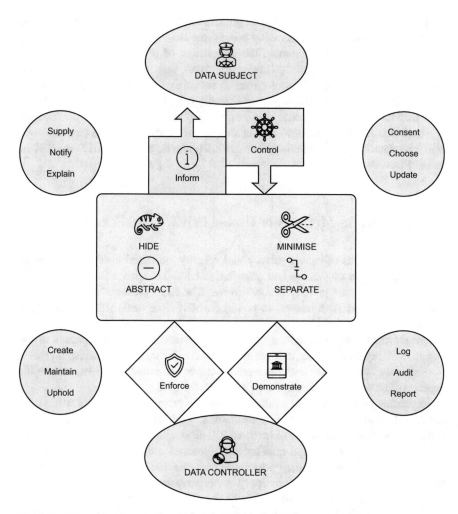

Fig. 5.12 Privacy design strategies (based on Bano et al. 2017)

are applied: summarising (finding and processing correlations instead of the data themselves), grouping (allocating data into common categories to avoid inducing detail on personal data before processing) and perturbing (adding noise[18]).

Informing refers to the provision of information to the data subject using three main tactics: supplying extensive resources about the processing of personal data, notifying about new information and explaining in concise and understandable form the information about data processing. Controlling is understood as the provision of data subjects with mechanisms to control the processing of their personal data. Three tactics are related to controlling: consenting, choosing and updating. From the

---

[18] See Mivule (2020) for an overview of noise usage in data privacy.

position of the data controllers, enforcing refers to the commitment and enforcement of a friendly personal data processing using three tactics: create while acknowledging the value of privacy, maintain the importance of privacy when designing or changing features and uphold. Threatening takes personal data as an asset and privacy as a goal. Demonstrating means to provide evidence of the treatment and processing of personal data in a privacy-friendly way. Logging (tracking processing data without revealing personal data), auditing (examining activities on risks for personal data and responding to discrepancies) and reporting are the tactics associated with demonstration. At this demonstration point, Bano et al. (2017) suggest the use of PIAs.

5.2 Evaluation Methods of Usable Privacy and Security

Evaluation methods of usable privacy and security are based upon usability techniques and include qualitative and quantitative empirical approaches similar to the first stages of the data privacy design process. The focus of the usable privacy and security evaluation is, however, to confirm whether the designed tools meet the defined targets or to determine possible usability failures regarding data privacy and security. Quantitative methods are commonly applied at the latest phases of the design, while qualitative methods are applied at the first stages of the design process (Rosenzweig 2015). However, both methods can be combined to understand specific aspects of the users' interactions with the tools, for example.

Regarding how to conduct evaluations, usable privacy and security distinguish between formative and summative evaluation. Formative evaluation insights on specific aspects of a prototype to improve it. The samples used in these evaluations are small (>10 persons), and qualitative approaches are applied. The summative evaluation focuses on comparing prototypes with established products or other kinds of benchmarks. These evaluations apply quantitative techniques in large population samples (Schaub and Cranor 2020). For testing different tasks, Rosenzweig (2015), based upon empirical experiences, recommends evaluating with a minimum of five persons for each task. For quantitative studies, a sample of 20 persons is recommended.

A common procedure in the evaluations is that a moderator conducts the tests following a script. The moderator interacts with the test participants to walk through the script and the designed tasks and collects information about the participants' behaviours. Frequently, the tasks are too many or too few in the real test situation. The moderator can let the participants play with the prototype and note the different interactions. In particular, the "thinking-aloud" technique focuses on these users "playing" with the prototypes (Rosenzweig 2015).

Best practices for usability testing include five steps (see Fig. 5.13). In the kick-off meeting before starting the tests, all the stakeholders and researchers make agreements about the schedules, benchmarks and deliverables. The researchers decided on the test design and the number of participants. In the planning step, the

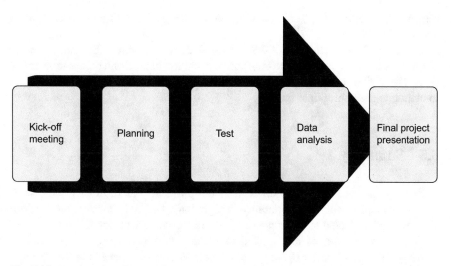

Fig. 5.13   Best practices for usability testing (based on Rosenzweig 2015)

Table 5.1   Standardised questionnaires for usability testing. Based on Sauro and Lewis (2016)

Questionnaires for administration after completing a set of test scenarios	Questionnaires for administration after completing a usability task or test scenario
The Questionnaire for User Interaction Satisfaction (QUIS)	The After-Scenario Questionnaire (ASQ)
The Software Usability Measurement Inventory (SUMI)	Expectation Ratings (ER)
The Post-Study System Usability Questionnaire (PSSUQ)	Usability Magnitude Estimation (UME)
The System Usability Scale (SUS)	The Single Ease Question (SEQ)
	The Subjective Mental Effort Question (SMEQ)

recruiting of participants starts, and a moderator's guide is approved. The tasks are also tested at this step to prepare for the next phase. Before the test phase starts, the instruments (moderator's guide, test system and tasks) are pilot tested. Then, after the positive pilot testing, the test phase begins. After completing all the tests, the data analysis takes place. The results and recommendations are written, followed by the final presentation of the project (Rosenzweig 2015).

Usability testing, including quantitative tests, frequently uses standardised and already validated questionnaires. There are a variety of standardised questionnaires for many different purposes. For example, Sauro and Lewis (2016) distinguish between questionnaires to be administered after a study and those used after testing a task or a scenario, as shown in Table 5.1.

Specifically, for usable privacy and security, best practices include the particular metrics for awareness and attention, discoverability, comprehension and utility of data privacy and security tools or features of a system as well as the usability dimensions of learnability, efficiency, memorability, errors and satisfaction (Schaub and Cranor 2020).

Applying these methods to OPS means evaluating whether the data subjects' privacy rights are covered by the transparency, choice, control and access tools in the OPS. The digital sovereignty aspects mentioned in the previous chapter can be used to elaborate the appropriate metrics.

5.3   Summary

- Privacy methods are based on privacy design principles (user centricity, relevance, understanding, actionability, integration). For OPS, these principles are specifically adapted to the contexts of use in e-government (see Chap. 2).
- Qualitative techniques are applied to directly understand users'/stakeholders' perspectives and needs (Rohrer 2014). Quantitative techniques aim to measure concrete defined aspects.
- Due to the interpretative nature of qualitative techniques focused on understanding users/stakeholders, the samples to apply these techniques are small and not representative. Quantitative techniques aim to measure defined features and may use representative samples.
- Planning and identifying specific user groups/stakeholders are necessary for both privacy impact assessment (PIA) and user experience (UX). In the case of OPS, this includes mapping out the information flows between the data subjects or citizens eligible for the public services and using them on the internet as well as business and public administrations and service providers (s. Chap. 4) and their concrete data privacy needs.
- Based on the results of the PIA/UX research, the design of data privacy and security tools using, among others, nudging methods takes place, followed by the evaluation phase.
- A common approach applied for the design of usable secure OPS is design thinking. Design thinking methods are based on the ideas of participatory design (Sanoff 2006), user-centred design (Norman 1988), service design (Kimbell 2010) and human-centred design (Gasson 2003), which confront the increasing integration and complexity of technological products and services in everyday life and the consequences of the disconnections between cultures and artefacts in the process of technological development.
- Several principles guide the implementation of design thinking methods: user focus, problem contextualisation, visualisation, diversity and experimentation (Carlgren et al. 2016).
- Design thinking usually comprises five phases: discovering or understanding the problem and users, interpreting the problem and user behaviour, generating ideas, experimenting with prototypes and developing or testing and improving.
- Design thinking methods can be used to increase the usability or usable security of e-government services such as user accounts together with citizens.

- Beyond participative methods for implementing usable secure OPS, the application of nudging methods (i.e. PETs) aims to change users' behaviour to enhance data privacy and security protection. While PETs have been criticised for their manipulative intentions,[19] the so-called transparency-enhancing technologies (TETs) emphasise the transparency aspect of usable privacy and security and particularly transparency, as it is included in the data privacy laws (i.e. GDPR) to build instruments that aim to support digital sovereignty.
- The focus of the usable privacy and security evaluation is to confirm whether the designed tools meet the defined targets or to determine possible usability failures regarding data privacy and security. For evaluation purposes, quantitative methods are commonly applied at the latest phases of the design, while qualitative methods are applied at the first stages of the design process (Rosenzweig 2015).

5.4 Examples and Exercises

5.4.1 Examples

A series of templates for service design methods is available at https://oecd-opsi.org/toolkits/service-design-toolkit/ (accessed 11 June 2023).

An example of applying design thinking for the development of public services is available at https://www.researchgate.net/publication/304344326_Bringing_Service_Design_Thinking_into_the_Public_Sector_to_Create_Proactive_and_User-Friendly_Public_Services (accessed 11 June 2023).

An example of a tool for evaluating the user centricity of e-government websites is available at Kamaruddin and Johari (2023).

5.4.2 Exercises (Work in Groups of Four Persons Max.):

- Develop a prototype of a digital identity wallet using paper and pencil and applying usable privacy and security criteria, design thinking methods and TETs.
- Evaluate the prototype by applying qualitative methods (focus group or interviews).
- A list of transparency requirements to match the GDPR is available at https://link.springer.com/chapter/10.1007/978-3-030-49443-8_8/tables/4 (accessed 11 June 2023).
- Online privacy tools are available at https://www.enisa.europa.eu/publications/privacy-tools-for-the-general-public (accessed 11 June 2023).

---

[19] See, for example, https://www.adalovelaceinstitute.org/blog/privacy-enhancing-technologies-not-always-our-friends/ (accessed 6 Jan 2023).

Glossary

Privacy-Enhancing Technologies (PETs) "Privacy Enhancing Technologies (PETs) are a suite of tools that can help maximise the use of data by reducing risks inherent to data use" [https://royalsociety.org/topics-policy/projects/privacy-enhancing-technologies/ (accessed 7 Mar 2023)].

Data Protection Impact Assessment (PIA) "A Data Protection Impact Assessment (DPIA) is a process to help you identify and minimise the data protection risks of a project" [https://ico.org.uk/for-organisations/guide-to-data-protection/guide-to-the-general-data-protection-regulation-gdpr/accountability-and-governance/data-protection-impact-assessments/ (accessed 7 Mar 2023)].

Transparency-Enhancing Technologies (TETs) "The goal of transparency enhancing tools (TETs) is to make the underlying processes more transparent, and to enable data subjects to better understand the implications that arise due to their decision to disclose personal data, or that have arisen due to choice made in the past" [https://www.diva-portal.org/smash/get/diva2:1119515/FULLTEXT02.pdf (accessed 7 Mar 2023)].

Further Reading

Hartzog W (2018) Privacy's blueprint: the battle to control the design of new technologies. Harvard University Press, Cambridge

Rosenzweig E (2015) Usability testing. In: Rosenzweig E (ed) Successful user experience: strategies and roadmaps, Chap 7, pp 131–154

Rossi A, Lenzini G (2020) Transparency by design in data-informed research: a collection of information design patterns. Comput Law Secur Rev 37:105402

References

Acquisti A, Adjerid I, Balebako R et al (2017) Nudges for privacy and security: understanding and assisting users' choices online. ACM Comput Surv 50(3):4

Albergotti A (2014) Facebook's Blue Dino wants you to mind your posting. WSJ Blog. http://blogs.wsj.com/digits/2014/04/01/facebooks-blue-dino-wants-you-to-mindyour-posting.   Accessed 30 Oct 2022

Alemanno A, Spina A (2014) Nudging legally: on the checks and balances of behavioural regulation. Int J Cons Law 12(2):429–456

Alsaghier H, Hussain R (2012) Conceptualization of trust in the e-government context: a qualitative analysis. In: Manohran A, Holzer M (eds) Active citizen participation in e-government: a global perspective. Information Science Reference, New York, pp 528–557

Alzahrani L, Al-Karaghouli W, Weerakkody V (2016) Analysing the critical factors influencing trust in e-government adoption from citizens' perspective: a systematic review and a conceptual framework. Int Bus Rev 26(1):164–175

Balboni P, Francis K (2022) Data protection as a corporate social responsibility. Maastricht University European Centre on Privacy & Cybersecurity, Maastricht

Bano S, Bassi E, Ciurcina M et al (2017) Privacy design strategies for the DECODE architecture. In: DECODE Project. DEcentralised Citizens Owned Data Ecosystem. Ref. Ares (2017)3294593 – 30/06/2017

Bason C (2010) Leading public sector innovation. Policy Press, Bristol

Bieker F (2022) The right to data protection. Individual and structural dimensions of data protection in EU law. Springer, Berlin

Brandimarte L, Acquisti A, Loewenstein G (2013) Misplaced confidences: privacy and the control paradox. Soc Psy Pers Sci 4(3):340–347

Bravo-Lillo C, Komanduri S, Cranor LF et al (2013) Your attention please: designing security-decision UIs to make genuine risks harder to ignore. In: Proceedings of the Symposium on Usable Privacy and Security (SOUPS'13). ACM, pp 1–12

Brignull H (2013) Dark Patterns: inside the interfaces designed to trick you. http://www.theverge.com/2013/8/29/4640308/dark-patterns-inside-the-interfaces-designed-to-trick-you. Accessed 3 May 2022

Brown T (2008) Design thinking. Harv Bus Rev 86(6):84–92

Braunstein A, Granka L, Staddon J (2011) Indirect content privacy surveys: measuring privacy without asking about it. In: Proceedings of the Seventh Symposium on Usable Privacy and Security (SOUPS '11). Association for Computing Machinery, New York, NY, Article 15, pp 1–14

Carlgren L, Rauth I, Elmquist M (2016) Framing design thinking: the concept in idea and enactment. Cre Inn Man 25(1):38–57

Colesky M, Hoepman JH, Hillen C (2016) A critical analysis of privacy design strategies. In: IEEE security and privacy workshops (SPW). IEEE, pp 33–40

Cordella A, Bonina CM (2012) A public value perspective for ICT enabled public sector reforms: a theoretical reflection. Gov Inf Quart 29(4):512–520

Dribbisch K (2016) Translating innovation. The adoption of Design Thing in a Singaporean Ministry. (Doctoral Thesis) Universität Potsdam. https://publishup.uni-potsdam.de/opus4-ubp/frontdoor/deliver/index/docId/10471/file/dribbisch_diss.pdf. Accessed 20 Apr 2022

Evans M, Terrey N (2016) Co-design with citizens and stakeholders. In: Evidence-based policy making in the social sciences. pp 243–262

Gao B, Berendt B, Clarke D, De Wolf R et al (2012) Interactive grouping of friends in OSN: towards online context management. In: Proceedings of the International Conference on Data Mining Workshops. IEEE, 555–562

Gasson S (2003) Human-centered vs. user-centered approaches to information system design. J Inf Technol Theory Appl 5(2):29–46

Goldstein DG, Johnson EJ, Herrmann A et al (2008) Nudge your customers toward better choices. Harv Bus Rev 86(12):99–105

Gov.UK (2022) Evidence review of Online Choice Architecture and consumer and competition harm. https://www.gov.uk/government/publications/online-choice-architecture-how-digital-design-can-harm-competition-and-consumers/evidence-review-of-online-choice-architecture-and-consumer-and-competition-harm. Accessed 20 Apr 2022

Gray CM, Kou Y, Battles B et al (2018) The dark (patterns) side of UX design. In: CHI 2018, April 21–26, 2018, Montréal, QC, Canada. https://dl.acm.org/doi/pdf/10.1145/3173574.3174108. Accessed 5 May 2022

Grossklags J, Acquisti A (2007) When 25 cents is too much: an experiment on willingness-to-sell and willingness-to-protect personal information. In: Proceedings of the Workshop on the Economics of Information Security (WEIS'07). pp 1–22

Gunawan J, Pradeep A, Choffnes D et al (2021) A comparative study of dark patterns across web and mobile modalities. In: Proceedings of the ACM on Human-Computer Interaction, 5 (CSCW2), pp 1–29

Hansen M (2008) Marrying transparency tools with user-controlled identity management. In: Fischer-Hübner S, Duquenoy P, Zuccato A, Martucci L (eds) The future of identity in the information society. Privacy and Identity 2007. IFIP — The International Federation for Information Processing, vol 262. Springer, Boston, MA

Hartzog W (2018) Privacy's blueprint: the battle to control the design of new technologies. Harvard University Press, Cambridge

Heuwing B, Maletz C (2019) Bürger-Services nutzerzentiert gestalten. In: Fischer H, Hess S (eds) Mensch und Computer 2019 – Usability Professionals. Gesellschaft für Informatik e.V. Und German UPA e.V., Bonn

Iaonnu A, Tussyadiha L, Miller G et al (2021) Privacy nudges for disclosure of personal information: a systematic literature review and meta-analysis. PLoS One. https://doi.org/10.1371/journal.pone.0256822

Ip E, Saeri A, Tear M (2018) Sludge: how corporations "nudge" us into spending more. The Conversation. https://theconversation.com. Accessed 2 May 2022

Johansson-Sköldberg U, Woodilla J, Çetinkaya M (2013) Design thinking: past, present and possible futures. Cre Inn Man 22(2):121–146

Kahneman D (2012) Thinking, fast and slow. Penguin Books, London

Kamaruddin KA, Johari NJ (2023) Is it citizen-centric? A tool for evaluating e-government websites' citizen-centricity. In: Yang XS, Sherratt S, Dey N, Joshi A (eds) Proceedings of Seventh International Congress on Information and Communication Technology. Lecture Notes in Networks and Systems, vol 448. Springer, Singapore. https://doi.org/10.1007/978-981-19-1610-6_32

Kelley PG, Cesca L, Bresee J, Cranor LF (2010) Standardizing privacy notices: an online study of the nutrition label approach. In: Proceedings of the Conference on Human Factors in Computing Systems (CHI'10). ACM, pp 1573–1582

Kimbell L (2010) From user-centered design to designing for services. In: Design Management Conference, London, pp 1–9

Kimbell L (2011) Rethinking design thinking: Part 1. Des Cul 3(3):285–306

Liedka J, Salzman R (2019) Applying design thinking to public service delivery. IBM Centre for the Business of Government. https://www.businessofgovernment.org/sites/default/files/Applying%20Design%20Thinking%20to%20Public%20Service%20Delivery.pdf.   Accessed 2 July 2022

Mathur A, Kshirsagar M, Mayer J (2021) What makes a dark pattern... dark?: Design attributes, normative considerations, and measurement methods. In: CHI '21: Proceedings of the 2021 CHI Conference on Human Factors in Computing Systems, May 2021, Article No.: 360, pp 1–18. https://arxiv.org/pdf/2101.04843.pdf. Accessed 16 May 2022

Mayoka K, Humphrey G (2016) A framework for usability of e-government services in developing countries. Glob Adv Res J Soc Sci 5:001–010. https://doi.org/10.5171/2017.313796

Mazzia A, LeFevre K, Adar E (2012) The PViz comprehension tool for social network privacy settings. In: Proceedings of the Symposium on Usable Privacy and Security (SOUPS'12). ACM, pp 1–12

Mills S (2020) Nudge/sludge symmetry: on the relationship between nudge and sludge and the resulting ontological, normative and transparency implications. Beh Pub Pol:1–24

Mivule K (2020) Utilizing noise addition for data privacy, an overview. https://arxiv.org/ftp/arxiv/papers/1309/1309.3958.pdf. Accessed 7 Feb 2023

Murmann P, Fischer-Hübner S (2017) Usable transparency enhancing tools – a literature review. Karlstadt University. https://www.diva-portal.org/smash/get/diva2:1119515/FULLTEXT02. Accessed 29 Nov 2022

Norman D (1988) The psychology of everyday things. Basic Books, London

Payne BD, Edwards WK (2008) A brief introduction to usable security. IEEE Internet Comput 12(3)

Pelkola D (2012) A framework for managing privacy-enhancing technology. IEEE Softw 29(3):45–49

Piasecki S (2017) "Schubs mich nicht!" – Nudging als politisches Gestaltungsmittel. https://www. bpb.de/lernen/digitale-bildung/werkstatt/258946/schubs-mich-nicht-nudging-als-politisches-gestaltungsmittel/. Accessed 13 Apr 2022

Rohrer C (2014) When to use which user-experience research methods. https://www.xdstrategy. com/wp-content/uploads/2018/08/When-to-Use-Which-User-Experience-Research-Methods-2014-10-12-Print.pdf. Accessed 24 Feb 2023

Rosenzweig E (2015) Usability testing. In: Rosenzweig E (ed) Successful user experience: strategies and roadmaps, Chap 7, pp 131–154

Rossi A, Lenzini G (2020) Transparency by design in data-informed research: a collection of information design patterns. Comput Law Secur Rev 37:105402

Rossi A, Palmirani M (2020) Can visual design provide legal transparency? The challenges for successful implementation of icons for data protection. Des Iss 36(3):82–96

Sanoff H (2006) Multiple views of participatory design. METU J Fac Arc 23(2):131–143

Sauro J, Lewis JR (2016) Quantifying the user experience: practical statistics for user research. Morgan Kaufmann, Burlington, MA

Schaub F, Cranor LF (2020) Usable and useful privacy interfaces. In: Breaux TD (ed) An introduction to privacy for technology professionals. IAPP

Schaub F, Balebako R, Durity A et al (2015) A design space for effective privacy notices. In: Proceedings of the Eleventh USENIX Conference on Usable Privacy and Security (SOUPS '15). https://www.usenix.org/conference/soups2015/proceedings/presentation/schaub. Accessed 3 Jan 2023

Seidel VP, Fixson SK (2013) Adopting design thinking in novice multidisciplinary teams: the application and limits of design methods and reflexive practices. J Pro Inn Man 30:19–33

Sunstein C (2019) Sludge ordeals. Duke Law J 68:1843–1883

Sunstein C (2020) Sludge audits. Beh Pub Pol:1–20

Thaler RH (2018) Nudge, not sludge. Editorial. In: Science. 431

Thouvenin F, Glatthaar M, Hotz J, Ettlinger C et al (2020) Privacy Icons: Transparenz auf einen Blick. In: Jusletter 30. November 2020

Trask A, Bluemke E, Garfinkel B et al (2020) Beyond privacy trade-offs with structured transparency. https://arxiv.org/ftp/arxiv/papers/2012/2012.08347.pdf. Accessed 5 Dec 2022

UN DESA (United Nations Department of Economic and Social Affairs) (2020) E-government survey 2020 digital government in the decade of action for sustainable development. With addendum on COVID-19 Response. New York. https://publicadministration.un.org/egovkb/Portals/egovkb/Documents/un/2020-Survey/2020%20UN%20E-Government%20Survey%20 (Full%20Report).pdf. Accessed 4 Jul 2022

Utz C, Degeling M, Fahl S et al (2019) (Un)informed Consent. In: Proceedings of the 2019 ACM SIGSAC Conference on Computer and Communications Security, pp 973–990

Verkijika SF, De Wet L (2018) A usability assessment of e-government websites in Sub-Saharan Africa. Int J Inf Man 39(C):20–29

Waldman AE (2020) Cognitive biases, dark patterns, and the 'privacy paradox' articles & chapters. 1332. https://digitalcommons.nyls.edu/fac_articles_chapters/1332. Accessed 17 Nov 2022

Wendel S (2016) Behavioral nudges and consumer technology. In: Abdukadirov S (ed) Nudge theory in action. Palgrave Advances in Behavioral Economics. Palgrave Macmillan, Cham

Zagal JP, Björk S, Lewis C (2013) Dark patterns in the design of games. In: Foundations of Digital Games 2013. Society for the Advancement of the Science of Digital Games, Santa Cruz, CA, 8. 34

Zimmermann C (2015) A categorization of transparency-enhancing technologies. https://arxiv.org/ftp/arxiv/papers/1507/1507.04914.pdf. Accessed Oct 3, 2023

Appendix:
Solutions for the Recommended Exercises

Chapter 1

1. **See page 7**: It focuses on the user by designing data protection and information security measures for IT products and services. User centricity and developers' awareness are central in this concept.
2. **See page 8**: Research in this area assumes that data privacy and security can be partially controlled from a user perspective through internal mechanisms or active engagement by users themselves, such as consent, correction or choice, as well as external instruments such as laws or technological self-regulation.
3. **See page 10**: Software developers and designers must therefore explore the reasons for security failures in the interactions between humans and computer systems. The privacy and security of information systems originally ignored the basic usability aspects of effectiveness, efficiency and satisfaction. These aspects have increasingly become important in the development of information systems and have led to the conceptualisation of usable privacy and security in academic and practitioner environments. If privacy and security of information systems ignore the skills and understandings of the users as well as the contexts of use, privacy and security can become a barrier to accomplishing basic systems requirements. This situation can lead to risks in which users may avoid activating security measures.
4. **See page 12**: In addition to these models of usable privacy and information security and trying to overcome the multidisciplinary contradictory interpretations about privacy and security in information systems, Lederer et al. (2004) propose to concentrate on the formulation of guidelines for designers of privacy and security. Lederer et al. identified five major privacy pitfalls grouped into two categories: first, understanding, including obscuring potential information flow and obscuring actual information flow, and second, action which includes an emphasis on configuration over action, lacks coarse-grained control and inhibits

E. Ruiz Ben, M. Scholl, *Usable Privacy and Security in Online Public Services*,
https://doi.org/10.1007/978-3-031-43383-2

established practice. To confront these pitfalls, Lederer et al. (2004) suggest different strategies, such as making explicit the basic scope of potential disclosures to help users understand their potential audience or informing users when someone else is locating them. Users learn with this strategy who is obtaining what information. Several guiding methods and tools have been developed and optimised for different contexts since these early stages of usable privacy and security with multidisciplinary contributions, for example, human-centred design, usability, security or psychology.

5. **See page 18/19**: PETs, privacy-enhancing technologies; TETs, transparency-enhancing technologies. In summary, usable privacy and security practices are supported by functionality tools (i.e. PETs and TETs nudges) to steer users into certain "safe" ways of use. While PETs can offer valuable mechanisms to protect users from unwanted data disclosure, they do not provide suitable support in the context of user profiling and personalisation in internet services characterised by high information asymmetry. TETs emphasise the transparency principle and provide users with information regarding providers' data collection, analysis and usage, aiming to reduce internet services' information asymmetry (Zimmermann 2015). An important aspect to consider in the implementation of these tools is their adaptation to different levels of users' competence and knowledge so that users can understand privacy mechanisms and security risks themselves and make informed choices. Mills (2022) proposes the personalisation of nudges to better acknowledge users' heterogeneity (Mills 2022).

Chapter 2

1. **See page 35:** Usability methods first help to identify the system requirements and further to confirm that the system meets those requirements under the basic criteria of efficiency, effectiveness, safety, utility, ease of learning, ease of remembering, ease of using and evaluating, practical visibility and usage satisfaction.

2. **See page 35:** In the specific context of e-government and more concretely in the development and implementation of online public services, these usability criteria should serve to confirm that online public services support citizens' digital sovereignty in terms of citizens' confidence in controlling, using and understanding digital facilities (BMWi 2021: 9).

3. **See page 35:** For designers of online public services, this means the need to include these usability criteria in their development agenda to enhance technology acceptance and performance and satisfy citizens' needs as well as those of public servants working in the delivery of public services.

4. **See page 60:** Table 2.4 SSI principles (s. Allen 2016)

Chapter 3

1. **See page 82:** Lawfulness, fairness, transparency, purpose limitation, data minimisation, accuracy, storage limitation, confidentiality and accountability
2. **See pages 83–84:** Table 3.1 Key aspects of the GDPR for public administrations

Chapter 4

1. **See page 100:** Citizens' digital sovereignty in the context of OPS requires a mutual awareness and dialogue between the state, the designers of the online public services and the citizens about forms of adoption and acceptance of digital services as well as about needs and responsibilities of the involved actors in the implementation and in data privacy and security. These are central usability topics. In the concrete context of e-government and OPS in the EU, the individual level of digital sovereignty (citizens and companies, as well as public administrations using OPS – soon mandatory through a single digital gateway) connects with the level of the state setting regulations and making decisions about technical solutions with economic partners (economic level) for delivering OPS in the EU.
2. **See page 102.**
3. **See page 104:** Comparing the privacy and security principles considered by these organisations, Multimukwe et al. (2019) have elaborated a classification in seven categories:

   - Notice and awareness
   - Access and user control
   - Storage limitation
   - Safeguard
   - Accuracy and security
   - Enforcement
   - Accountability

Two of these categories, notice and awareness and access and user control, are particularly connected to usable privacy and security (how to give access to online services and inform about data privacy and security in an effective, efficient and satisfactory way for the data subjects).

References

Allen C (2016) The path to self-sovereign identity. Life with Alacrity. https://www.lifewithalacrity.com/2016/04/the-path-to-self-sovereign-identity.html. Accessed 10 Jan 2023

BMWi (Bundesministerium für Wirtschaft und Energie) (2021) Digitale Souveränität Bestandsaufnahme und Handlungsfelder. BMWi and ZEW Mannheim

Lederer S, Hong J, Dey A et al (2004) Personal privacy through understanding and action: five pitfalls for designers. Carnegie Mellon University

Mills S (2022) Personalized nudging. Behav Public Policy 6(1):150–159

Multimukwe C, Kolkowska E, Grönlund A (2019) Information privacy practices in e-government in an African least developing country, Rwanda. E J Info Sys Dev Countries 85:2

Zimmermann C (2015) A categorization of transparency-enhancing technologies. https://arxiv.org/ftp/arxiv/papers/1507/1507.04914.pdf. Accessed Oct 3, 2023

Printed in the United States
by Baker & Taylor Publisher Services